NUTRITION FOR YOUR SOUL

Because Man Does Not Live by Bread Alone…

REBECCA BASSHAM

Published by
Edge Neuro Fitness, LLC.
1990 McCulloch Blvd. #D276
Lake Havasu City, AZ 86403
edgeneurofitness.com

Nutrition for Your Soul:
Because Man Does Not Live by Bread Alone
Copyright © 2020 by Rebecca Bassham

Cover design & interior layout by
Hyperspace Internet Technologies, Inc.

All rights reserved. No part of this book may be used or reproduced in any manner whatsoever without written permission except in the case of brief quotations embodied in critical articles and reviews.

For information please address Rebecca Bassham.
bec@edgeneurofitness.com

Library of Congress Control Number: 2020924456
ISBN (e-book) 978-0-578-81565-7
ISBN (paperback) 978-0-578-81564-0

Dedication

This book is dedicated to God, who has been with me; always and forever. And to those who seek refuge, hope, strength, and the fuel to carry on.

CONTENTS

FOREWORD vii
PREFACE ix
INTRODUCTION xv
Chapter 1   Character-Building Opportunities 1
Chapter 2   Inside Out 7
Chapter 3   Shelter 13
Chapter 4   Something's Fishy 19
Chapter 5   "Glory!" 23
Chapter 6   Is it Sunday? 29
Chapter 7   James 1…The First Sentence 33
Chapter 8   James vs. Stormy Trials 35
Chapter 9   It's Tempting 39
Chapter 10 Leadership 43
Chapter 11 Proverbs 31:10-31…The Virtuous Woman 49
Chapter 12 Song of a Desert Romance 57
Chapter 13 Recipe for Fruit 59
Chapter 14 Scoop or Poop 65
Chapter 15 Humble Pie 71
Chapter 16 Humble Pie Part II…The Next Step 79

Chapter 17 Spooky 83
Chapter 18 Testing, Testing 87
Chapter 19 When Good Things Happen to Bad People 93
Chapter 20 Are You Ready for Christmas? 97
Chapter 21 Happy New Year! 103
Chapter 22 Peace Out 107
Chapter 23 Marching Orders 113
Chapter 24 It's Your Turn 119
ACKNOWLEDGEMENTS 121
ABOUT THE AUTHOR 125

FOREWORD

Perspicacity refers to a penetrating discernment, a clarity of vision or intellect which provides a deep understanding and insight. In her book, Nutrition for Your Soul, Bec has used a penetrating discernment to examine the obstacles we all confront in some manner that stand in our way to health and equanimity. Through many personal stories, a very deep faith and in-depth knowledge and familiarity with scripture and deep personal reflection, she shares with the reader simple but profound stories. Chapters range from character-building opportunities to why bad things happen to good people. The uplifting stories, the humorous anecdotes and the powerful biblical quotes and admonitions provide a smorgasbord of food for thought for all and true "Nutrition for the Soul."

Joseph C. Maroon, MD, FACS

Clinical Professor and Vice Chairman Heindl Scholar in Neuroscience Department of Neurosurgery University of Pittsburgh, Team Neurosurgeon, The Pittsburgh Steelers, Medical Director, World Wrestling Entertainment

PREFACE

*Man does not live by bread alone.
(Deut. 8:3).*
We must feed our souls as well. My point is not to argue the fact that we all have a mind, body, brain, and soul. The focus here is on our souls.

The **body** must be nourished and exercised. The **mind** benefits from healthy food, solid education, mental exercise, and stimulation. Have you ever heard the phrase, "sharpen the saw?" So, it is with your **soul**. *Heb. 4:12 For the Word of God is living and active. Sharper than any double-edged sword, it penetrates even to dividing soul and spirit, joints, and marrow, it judges the thoughts and attitudes of the heart.* The soul is your immaterial, spiritual essence, which is contained within the human nature of your physical being. Intelligence, personality, and emotional control reflect the state of your mental health and capabilities. Likewise, temperament, disposition, attitude, and frame of mind reflect the status of your soul, or spiritual health.

In my life I have met people that appear to be like walking dead, going through the motions of life, but not "alive." Have you ever felt like a dark cloud was hovering above you, "foggy", or lost? I have. **Rom. 8:28 And we know that in all things God works for the goal of those who love him, who have been called according to His purpose.** God, in his infinite, eternal wisdom, will give us purpose and meaning. But how? Just turn to Him. That is the purpose of this book; to connect the dots, one line at a time.

Just like with good food or a good education, we do not fill up all at once. It happens one bite or step at a time. We do not remain full, rather we burn it off as energy, fueling our lives and imparting into the lives of others, just ask any mother or teacher! Hence, we must refuel, to avoid "running on empty," or starving our spirit.

What I offer in this book is a pantry of encouraging words, some directly from and some directing to the Bible, or God's cupboard so to speak. *His words bring me life!* **John 14:6 Jesus answered, "I am the way, the truth, and the life."** My goal is to help the reader fill his or her soul, to keep it full, and ultimately teach others how they can do the same. **Ps. 73:28 But as for me, it is good to be near God. I have made the Sovereign Lord my refuge; I will tell of all your deeds.**

It started years ago, when someone encouraged me to read a chapter of the Bible every day then write down answers to the following three questions,

1. What part of the chapter stood out the most to you?
2. Why?
3. How will I apply it to my life?

This led to a pile of readings which offered a storehouse of wisdom, lessons, and history. The history was not just Biblical, but personal through its application to my life. Going through this process, it became evident to me how the Bible is "living and active".

My entire career has involved being a health educator; lecturing, health and life coaching, personal training, promoting organic living and nutrition, and in practice as a psychophysiologist to foster the awareness and application of the mind-body connection. It became a way of life. The importance of nutrition, exercise, and mental wellness is commonly understood and covered well in the media. Furthermore, the mind, body, brain, and soul have an interdependent relationship and must be in **balance** for our most optimal health.

It occurred to me that I ought to share my spiritual journal to bridge the gap between the physical and spiritual realms. If I can help people with exercise, nutrition, and cognitive skills, I can surely offer something to enrich their souls. My notes were saved over the years, and gradually grew into a spiritual treasure trove. In the process, I hope to leave a legacy of wisdom, memories, tears, prayers, testimonies, encouragement, and even laughter for anyone who dares to turn the pages and actually read the many words inside this collection of "food for your soul."

The reader will explore stories about lessons learned while navigating through life experiences as a wife, mother, coach, businesswoman, and friend. Indeed, many of us have the same type of experiences. I like to call them "character-building opportunities!" Sometimes I muddled or slipped back, but after taking the time to seek God for His Word, I always emerged stronger, and one step closer to fulfillment and peace.

The following Chapters turned into a series of devotional steppingstones with Biblical references. They brought me closer to God as I traveled the journey along my spiritual path. Oh, I do not claim to be "there" yet, that is not until I arrive in Heaven! Occasionally I wander off the path, but then remember who I am in Christ with a return to my notes for review and personal reflection. The notes feed my soul. They inspire me to get back on track. Hopefully, you will be inspired, too, and eventually inspire yourself with a journal challenge or "recipe" at the end of the book.

I promise you a delightful assortment of chapters as *Nutrition for Your Soul*. Consider them as little snacks to uplift and feed your spirit any time of day or night. My hope is that you get to know the Lord as I know Him, for He can nourish and sustain you like nothing else in this material world.

Please accept my encouragement, dear reader, feed your soul every day. *Read one chapter of this book each day for the next twenty-one days. Studies show that it takes 21 days to form a new habit. Feeding your soul is a good habit!* Allow this platter of nourishment to pour from my soul to yours. Enjoy the sweet taste of good spiritual food. Chew on it, swallow, digest, and absorb it. Because you took the time to read the following pages, may you be nourished, strengthened, blessed, entertained, encouraged, and filled.

My challenge to you is to read just one chapter a day. Pray about it, and ask yourself if there are applications to your life.

At the end of the book, you will have the opportunity create your own recipe. I also encourage you to share. Dr. William Sears says, "Success is not measured by the amount of money you make, but by the amount of people you help." God will help you as well if you will only let him, then listen to what **He** says. He will nourish your soul. This book is just to whet your appetite!

Are you hungry? Welcome to my kitchen

Bec
Also Known As "The Brain DJ"

INTRODUCTION

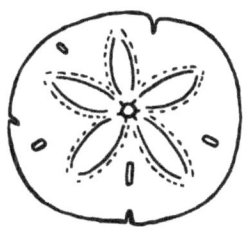

Food for Thought

Each chapter of this book provides a portion of spiritual food, which concludes with a couple of food for thought questions. The intent of this introspection is to offer an opportunity to reflect on the reading. Ask yourself how it may apply to you or come up with your own conclusions. It is easy to skim over this portion or simply give the question a little thought. But investing a few or more minutes to willfully put the answers to pen and paper, honor them, and give them a voice can yield a deeper connection to your soul, to God, and your inner consciousness.

The act of writing is the important part, no matter how messy, no matter the grammar. Messy can indicate something is really happening here, like a tidal wave of emotional or spiritual processing. This is not English class. You will not be judged. The answers are solely between you and God. You can ask Him for words and insight. The hardest part is just getting started. That first stroke of the pen is all it takes. Just show up on the page and allow God to speak to you. I promise, He will be there if you call upon Him. He wants to hear from you. Your voice matters. Listen for Him as he responds to you on the page. It is a great way to communicate, sometimes even easier than prayer as it can help focus by directing thought to the page. Just watch what happens…

That is how this book happened! Someone challenged me to put my thoughts on one page every morning. Just read the short chapter, meditate on his words, show up on the page, and allow it to happen. No trying. Just allow. Let it happen, and let it flow, whatever comes out. Breathe. I'm praying for you.

CHARACTER-BUILDING OPPORTUNITIES

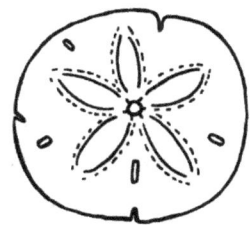

Romans 5:2b-4 And we rejoice in the hope of the glory of God. Not only so, but we also rejoice in our sufferings, because we know that suffering produces perseverance; perseverance, character; and character, hope.

Who likes to suffer? Rejoice in it? Not me! God uses suffering, however, to move us on to produce perseverance and expand character. It is written that we are to assume the character of Christ. He certainly suffered, but God was with him. Likewise, God is with us, **Rom. 5;5 And hope does not disappoint us, because God has poured out his love into our hearts by the Holy Spirit, whom he has given us.** God's love in us will give us the ability to love and live through the suffering experience. He knows we cannot do it on our own accord. I once heard Greg Laurie say in a sermon that when Satan came knocking on his door, he answered, "Hey God! Can you get that?" This is a demonstration of letting God and His love, help us respond to adversity.

1 Cor. 3:9 For we are God's fellow workers; you are God's field, God's building. God has a stake in the matter! He uses us to do *his* work for *his* glory, so of course he wants us to succeed. He never promised it would be easy or without suffering, but hard work is worth the effort. And God promises to complete the work he began in us. ***Phil 1:6 He who began a good work in you will carry it on to completion until the day of Christ Jesus.*** Remember this is a process, it takes time, and He is not through with you yet. You are His building project, His creation. We can choose to continue building our character by focusing on a positive outcome rather than on our suffering. That's a tall order. I want to be tall, not small, to grow in my faith and spirit. It usually requires fellowship with other Christians to grow.

In Phil. 1:5, Paul begins his letter by describing how he ***always prays with joy because of your partnership in the gospel.*** The Philippians, in essence, were his "partners in the gospel." It helps to pair up by having a prayer/accountability partner. We cannot always depend on others to pray for all our needs, we must also take part on our own behalf. On the other hand, we need not be "lone rangers". Check out what Jesus said to his disciples in the book of Matthew, ***Mat. 18:19-20 "Again, I tell you that if two of you on earth agree about anything you ask for, it will be done for you by my father in heaven. For where two or three come together in my name, there am I with them."*** Fellowship can be powerful. You may be better off if you don't try to face a situation alone.

One day I had a revelation that I could view my "situations" and "issues" as "opportunities," *character-building opportunities.*

Rather than saying to myself, "Spit happens!" or "This stinks!" I can choose to say, "This would be a character-building opportunity!" Consider the situation as a crossroads, a test, and a chance to learn a lesson. In school, we learn a lesson, take a test, and move to the next level if we pass. We come out a little smarter in the end. After hard work, we usually become stronger. And, as Paul describes in the book of Romans, we can also become stronger in our spirit. At times, however, it may seem as if things just are not going anywhere.

Did you ever seem to be stuck in a rut? These are the times when God is trying to communicate, "Hello? Remember me?" During these times, I usually have a conversation with God that goes something like this, "God, help! I need a clue! I don't get it! What are you trying to tell me? What do you want me to do?" Of course, at this point, it's necessary to stop and listen for an answer. It can take time and effort, most things worthwhile do. Keep seeking Him until you get that clue, pray about it, and make sure it lines up with His Word. Then kick off the cement shoes that are holding you down, put on your "PF Flyers", and spring into action! We can choose to build character for God's glory by walking in love and walking in His way when in the throes of a rut or a storm.

Oh, you don't have to get it right all the time. God is patient. He is the spirit of love and gives us many second chances. As He loves and forgives us, likewise, we should love and forgive others, which brings us back to opportunities. Let's see what the Bible says about these opportunities…

Gal. 6:10 Therefore, as we have opportunity, let us do good to all people, especially to those who belong to the family of believers.

Col. 4:5-6 Be wise in the way you act toward outsiders; make the most of every opportunity. Let your conversation be always full of grace, seasoned with salt, so that you may know how to answer everyone.

That appears crystal clear to me. It does not say to bury your head in the sand, whine, curse ("pepper") the situation, make excuses, or run away. It looks like we should be good to believers and outsiders, make the most of it, and respond with wisdom and grace (salt). That's another tall order. I'm sure glad God is there to help! I'm also thankful for all the tools like church, fellowship, and Bible study. I could never come up with this on my own. My mission here is to show you what I have learned so far through my own adversity and study, for what it's worth!

Now let's go back to Paul's prayer in **Phil. 1:9-11** *"And this is my prayer: that your love may abound more and more in knowledge and depth of insight, so that you may be able to discern what is best and may be pure and blameless until the day of Christ, filled with the fruit of righteousness that comes through Jesus Christ- to the glory and praise of God."* Personally, I would rather be full than empty. Filled with love, wisdom, insight, and good stuff, not bitter, confused, and bleh! Is that a word? I'm referring to that bad stuff for lack of a more appropriate word in this case. Several words I should not use just flew through my head, just being honest.

I challenge you to go to the filling station daily. Consider **what** is filling you, **where** filling station is, and go to God for the good stuff. Do not wait until the gauge reads empty. Someone may have to stop what they are doing to tow or carry you along. Fill up! Maybe consider carrying an extra "can of gas" to help someone else, now I'm thinking of my AAA card. I can call a number on my card for insurance that a professional will give me roadside assistance or give me a map to my destination.

As Christians, we have a similar plan. It is the insurance of salvation. The Bible is our road map to character building. Our belief is the card, a gift. It never expires. Thoughts like this make my road a little easier and more meaningful to travel. Now let us move on to the next lesson.

Food for thought:
Describe a recent "character-building opportunity" in your life.

Would you do anything different next time?

INSIDE OUT

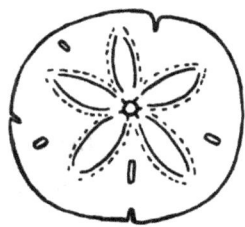

Chances are, you have probably heard it said, 'It does not matter what's on the outside, but on the inside that counts.' I agree for the most part. No matter how beautiful you are, ugliness on the inside will appear on the outside, reflected on your face, in your expression, or how you carry yourself. Beauty is more than skin deep.

My teenage daughter is a striking beauty, but oh my, when she is angry, she is downright scary to look at! "Girl, you're being so ugly!" "I'm not ugly!" she retorts with a huffy noise. I say, "You're acting ugly and it makes you look bad." Me, too... PMS and menopause do not mix. Have you heard that one? How about this one, "Mirror, mirror on the wall..." Take a look at **Psalm 34:5 Those who look to him are radiant; their faces are never covered with shame.** Think of this radiance as being "Son-burned!" Does your face reflect Jesus, or just yourself?

Mat. 23:25 "Woe to you, teachers of the law and Pharisees, you hypocrites! You clean the outside of the cup and dish, but on the inside, they are full of greed and self- indulgence. Just like the average teenage girl who spends hours in front of the mirror primping, wears clothes to reflect their fashion status, and tries to conform within the customs of a certain social structure, the Pharisees, too, were overly concerned with their outward appearance, rigid regulations, and social hierarchy. God looks at the inside, in our hearts. Often, no matter what someone looks like or appears to be on the outside, you can sense it when something does not line up or is wrong on the inside. Other times you cannot tell the outside from the inside, like a box of chocolates. They all look tasty on the outside, but you never know what you're going to get on the inside.

I recall one day in particular, years ago, preparing my three preschool- aged children to attend our weekly Bible study, thinking I had it all together. They were fed, dressed, and the diaper bag was packed, whew! My independent little daughter, less than two years old at the time, insisted upon dressing herself. As we were leaving, I noticed her shirt revealed evidence of breakfast on it. Oh no, not much time to change… but alas, she had put it on inside out. I simply took it off, turned it outside in (which was really the inside in, along with the unsightly stain) and we were good to go. Cool! I do not think a food stain inside the shirt of a small child really mattered to God. What mattered is that we all arrived at our study on time. We came in presentable.

Now let us step into the kitchen… when serving a meal, presentation can be significant. A creative chef will take some ordinary or even "yukky, healthy" food and transform it into an awesome appetizing adventure with some thoughtful flair of presentation. I used to make funny faces and such with vegetables and fruits. Who says you cannot play with your food? If you eat well (and you're at home, of course!) I still do!

Check out my little Valentine platter. The presentation made it look good enough to eat. That same food on a regular plate would have turned away my family if I were trying to bless them with a special treat. Well these foods really ARE a blessing, full of nutritional goodness on the inside, but on the outside, they appear to be the same old boring fruits and veggies I usually must strongly persuade, force, or manipulate them to eat. See, in this case, the inside and the outside mattered. Hooked by my little presentation, they took the bait, and I scored! This kitchen nutrition mission succeeded.

2 Tim. 2:15 Do your best to present yourself to God as one approved, a workman who does not need to be ashamed and who correctly handles the word of truth. Now here is a case where the outside matters. As ambassadors of Christ, we should look appropriate and shameless. It does not mention anything about perfection, does it? I especially like the "do your best" part. Sounds manageable, palatable. We must also carefully select God's precious Words of truth, not using them inappropriately, out of context, or altering them.

2 Tim. 3:16 All scripture is God-breathed and is useful for teaching, rebuking, correcting and training in righteousness, so that the man of God may be thoroughly equipped for every good work. Here we can take words from the inside of our Bible, bring them out and use them for His good purpose. Now that has potential for making our work look prettier.

Inside out. Sometimes it matters, sometimes not. It could be our appearance, choice of words, our situations. It could be anything in life. Some things matter, some not, some on the inside, some on the outside. Hmmm… that sounds complicated and makes me think. Often, it is good to contemplate and think things through. It can serve you well to pray about all that stuff, too. God hears our prayers about everything. Then there are those times when it is best to just let it go. My grandmother used to say, "Give it to God." Did you ever want to take something off your plate?

Phil: 4:6: Do not be anxious about anything, but in EVERYTHING, by prayer and petition, with thanksgiving, present your requests to God.

1 John 5:14-15: This is the confidence we have on approaching God: that if we ask anything according to his will, he hears us. And if we know that he hears us—whatever we ask—we know that we have what we asked of him.

Note the part in 1 John about "His will." What really matters is what *matters* to God, but most of that happens on the inside, doesn't it? Eventually it shows up on the outside. I will keep my eyes open. I will keep asking God to help me see things as He does, to show me what matters, and to reveal things from the inside out. He is much better at figuring out these things than I am.

Food for thought:
Describe a time when you felt inside out.

What really mattered the most?

SHELTER

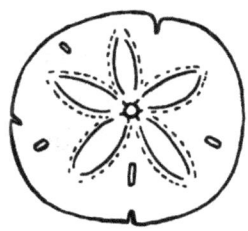

Ps. 91:1-2 He who dwells in the shelter of the Most High will rest in the shadow of the Almighty. I will say of the Lord, "He is my refuge and my fortress, my God, in whom I trust." According to Webster's New Collegiate Dictionary, the definition of *dwell* is *to remain for a time, to live as a resident, to keep the attention directed.* With this thought in mind, Psalm 91 took on a new meaning for me. I read it one morning, skimming hurriedly across the words. The next day I re-read it. A light bulb suddenly turned on in my brain! Dwell. Stay there, not just physically, but mentally. I asked myself the following questions: "Where do you dwell? Where does your heart lie? Where does your head lie?" Most important, "Where is your soul focused?"

You see, I had a rough day, two days to be precise, and it was not over yet! In the throes of a "character-building opportunity, or CBO", my mind had been spinning, feathers ruffled, and my soul was not peaceful. Back to Psalm 91. These words offered hope, comfort, and direction. Isn't that what we all need in times of conflict and distress? While the situation remained, I felt stronger, knowing what to do different that day rather than spinning and ruffling. Personally, I do not like the spinning and ruffling stuff because it's exhausting, especially for more than a few minutes at a time. And my hair gets real messed up, too!

I remember sitting in the bleachers watching the last part of the basketball game my daughter was cheering for, wanting to hide, wondering what people might be thinking of me, thinking to myself, "What a mess I am! Oh, who cares? I'll look better the next game (another chance tomorrow) and have a great story of triumph to share about how my dignity was restored." Then, silently, I told God, "I'm standing on that one, Lord!" How was it possible to move through this "CBO", changing gears from "spinning out there and ruffled" to rested and at peace?

Here is how it happened. Starting with the word *dwell*, I read Psalm 91. For two days straight, I dwelled in upheaval. Sure, both my thoughts and prayers were about God and His power to help me, still, even this was not enough do my part to really reap the harvest! Failure to do the next part, which was to *rest in the shadow of the Almighty*, left me in turmoil, without rest, spinning and ruffling, whew! I continued trying to comfort myself by clearing my head, getting some fresh air, walking the dogs, riding my horses, calling the pastor, and calling a friend. God's Word was the missing ingredient needed to complete the recipe for success. Psalm 91 nourished and comforted my soul once I went there, finally coming to rest securely in the shadow of the Almighty. In order to remember the footprints to follow, I wrote down the following directions so anyone could find their way to refuge.

The **first** turn you make is to the "shelter." Have you ever felt or been told that you were "out there?" Ever been caught out in the rain? I don't know about you, but I head for shelter. Now look at **verses 3-6: *Surely, he will save you from the fowler's snare and from the deadly pestilence. He will cover you with his feathers, and under his wings you will find refuge; his faithfulness will be your shield and rampart. You will not fear the terror of night, not the arrow that flies by day, nor the pestilence that stalks in the darkness, nor the plague that destroys at midday.*** God will cover and protect you. All you must do is ask. ***Luke 11:10 For everyone who asks, receives, he who seeks, finds; and to him who knocks, the door will be opened.*** So, there is a way in and an open door. The soulful shelter can be found upon turning thoughts around to dwell on God's Words. It was not enough just to call the pastor and pray. I needed to seek refuge in the "shelter" to spend some time with God, listening.

The **second** step is to go IN the shelter. Stay there until the storm is over. I can't necessarily stay in my prayer corner (which is actually a comfy corner of my couch) all day, but can write His Words on an index card and carry them along all day for quick reference, striving to memorize them, hiding these words in my heart. ***Ps.119:11 I have hidden your words in my heart that I might not sin against you.*** This is like a spiritual GPS so you can get back to the shelter from wherever you happen to be, because shelter is good when you are in a storm! I like the part about covering with feathers (nice and fluffy like a down pillow) and being under his wings. Rather than flapping mine, I can rest under His! They are bigger and stronger. Mine are tired.

The psalm goes on to describe how in the shelter, you will not fear, you will observe others falling at your side, and the wicked get punished. ***V. 7-13 A thousand may fall at your side, ten thousand at your right hand, but it will not come near you. You will only observe with your eyes and see the punishment of the wicked. If you make the Most High your dwelling—even the Lord, who is my refuge—then no harm will befall you, no disaster will come near your tent. For he will command his angels concerning you to guard you in all your ways; they will lift you up in their hands, so that you will not strike your foot against a stone. You will tread upon the lion and the cobra; you will trample the great lion and the serpent.***

If you make God your dwelling, He promises that no harm will befall you, no disaster will come near your tent, and his angels will guard and lift you up. These are some powerful words! He is a big God whose boundaries are wide. It even mentions your feet… that you will not strike your foot against a stone, and you will tread upon lions and serpents. Perhaps that means he will guide your path and the enemy, while not necessarily wild beasts but those who come against you, will be on the bottom of your shoes!

Verse 14 "Because he loves me," says the Lord, "I will rescue him; I will protect him, for he acknowledges my name." Here we see a cost. The admission ticket to the shelter is the love and acknowledgement of God. Everyone can afford that. It's an allocation thing. ***Mat. 6:24 "No one can serve two masters. Either he will hate the one and love the other, or he will be devoted to the***

one and despise the other. You cannot serve both God and Money. Love God or love money. Choose to be "out there" or under his cover. No dollar amount is given here. The issue is where your love is spent.

Oh, how I love the shelter, the Word, the Lord. What a good place to be.

Ps. 91:15-16 "He will call upon me, and I will answer him; I will be with him in trouble, I will deliver him and honor him. With long life will I satisfy him and show him my salvation." Sounds like a nice place to dwell. When I call out for God, I want to hear him. I'm looking for answers. I do not want to be alone in my troubles, I want deliverance, and prefer to come out of it in honor rather than disgrace, with a long satisfying life that ends in salvation. This only happens within his shelter. I will stay there, dwell. Oh dwell…

Thank you Lord for your shelter, for the shadow of your protection, the comfort and lift of your feathered wings in my storm, and the answers you will provide as I call out to you. The victory is all for your glory.

Food for thought:
Where do you head during a "storm?"

Describe how you feel while in there.

How about when you come out?

SOMETHING'S FISHY
Lessons from Jonah 1

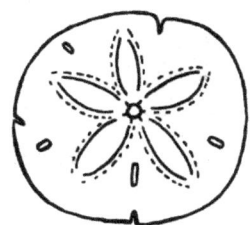

God told Jonah to go to Ninevah to preach there about the wickedness going on. Jonah did not follow God's directions. He made other plans for himself and ran away to a more pleasant place called Tarshish. The first thing that occurred to me when I began to read this story is, "Jonah, does *omnipresence* mean anything to you? As if God did not know where you were."

Ps. 139:7 Where can I go from your Spirit? Where can I flee from your presence?

Josh. 1:5 I will never leave you nor forsake you. To me, this means God watches over you everywhere, anywhere. He does not give up on you either. Jonah gave up on God's plan and set sail for Tarshish.

Jonah did not get far. A great storm brewed upon them. Even the crew knew this was not just any ordinary storm. This storm was so big it prevented him from going in the wrong direction. It did not stop the ship at first. They kept trying to ride it out. Jonah even slept through it for a while until the crew woke him up. They cast lots to find out who was responsible, knowing there had to be a reason for such an upheaval. "Who did it?" they asked. God told them it was Jonah. Busted. ***Jonah 1:8 "What do you do? Where do you come from? What is your country, from what people are you?"*** These are all valid questions. Maybe they should have asked him, "Why are you going there? What's your plan?" The crew did not ask questions until it was too late to avoid the storm.

Have you ever been the innocent victim of calamity while on a journey of some sort? Often, we can avoid tragedy by taking a moment to consider **who** hops on board with us. Who are you traveling through life with? I recall a couple of planes that crashed into the World Trade Center on 9/11. Somebody did not ask enough questions before allowing those terrorists on board. That was another lesson learned too late. Much too late.

Getting back to the story of Jonah, after the revelation, Jonah said, ***v.12 "Pick me up and throw me into the sea, it will become calm. I know that it is my fault that this great storm has come upon you."*** Following some debate and hesitation, they threw him overboard, then the raging sea calmed. At least he did not fight it! He went willingly. God gave him half credit for that one and sent him a great fish to live in for three days.

Inside the belly of a whale, what a "time out." It usually stinks when we land in between where we want to go and where God wants us to be. I don't even want to go there with whale belly atmospheric conditions. I have been in some undesirable places, but never there! Maybe if you are in an undesirable place, it's time to consider how you got there, where you should be, and ask God how to get out of it. He will tell you...

John 15:7 If you remain in me and my words remain in you, ask whatever you wish, and it will be given to you. That is what Jonah did for those three days.

Like Jonah, I never seem to get far when I stray out along my own path. It becomes "stormy". Most of our "storms of life" result from bad choices made upon charting our course, or failure to do so. In essence, we choose to go there. And not to decide really is to decide not to address a thing and just allow it to happen or "go there" generically. Within the book of Deuteronomy lie many blessings for obedience to the Lord along with curses for disobedience. Let us visit here for a while. Time and again throughout the Old Testament we see stories of blessing and curses, obedience, and rebellion. I have seen it in and lived through it my own life, have you? Here is a promise from God:

Deut. 28:1-2 If you fully obey the Lord your God and carefully follow all his commands I give you today, the Lord your God will set you high above all the nations on earth. All these blessings will come upon you and accompany you if you obey the Lord your God. v.6 You will be blessed when you come in and blessed when you go out.

I will hitch a ride on that promise! Want to come on board?

Food for thought:
Describe someone who seemed "fishy" to you.

Did you ever try to hide from God?

If so, how did that work?

Thank God for loving you wherever you are and ask Him where he wants you to be.

"GLORY!"

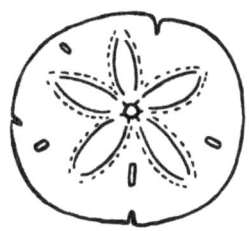

Psalm 62:11-12 "One thing God has spoken, two things have I heard: that you, O God, are strong, and that you, O Lord, are loving. Surely you will reward each person according to what he has done."

Awesome! These verses bring life and joy to my soul. Here is why. I could say, "Glory!" instead. A dear pastor friend of mine who passed on to his eternal life used the word "glory" all the time when he got excited about a Bible verse or a praise report. I will never forget the expression of joy on his face when he shared. That is because these "awesome" words and awesome good reports bring forth glory. Stay with me and I will show you how it works.

The first thing I notice in this psalm is that God *spoke* and David, the writer, *heard*. Amen! I pray for my family every day, that God will speak to them and they will hear it, just like David did. Oh, **I** hear God, especially when I take the time to listen, pay attention, and be aware of what He is telling me. It really helps to focus.

The "School of Hard Knocks" taught me over the years that I cannot navigate through life, without taking some time to focus on God. I learned to be concerned with the spiritual and temporal welfare of my family. Helping our families become aware of God's presence in their life is a daily challenge. But this challenge is not met or well received through nagging. Nagging often results in resistance! Gentle guidance, prayer, and a creative expression of God's Love make the best formula for success in the matter by allowing God to take over and direct us along the path He wants us to follow as well as to lead our families.

God is *strong (v.12)* and powerful. His strength outweighs any of our problems, even prodigal, wayward children. **Ps. 18:1-2 "The Lord is my rock, my fortress, and my deliverer; my God is my rock, in whom I take refuge. He is my shield and the horn of my salvation, my stronghold."** Those words make me feel strong. Glory! Do you feel something happening here? I feel weak when I try to take on life's challenges on my own accord but looking at God's words and turning my thoughts toward Him restores my strength. Where we are weak, He is strong. We can go on another day relying on His strength… and His WORDS! Not our own words or philosophical or pop psychology words… but Holy Spirit breathed timeless promise Words. These really came in handy when my oldest son rebelled as a teenager. It was hard to come up with the right words for him. It required help and inspiration to communicate with him wisely but on a level of teenage understanding.

God's words are full of love. God IS love and we can love through Him, with His help. Like navigating through life, loving is another thing we cannot always do without Him. We may find ourselves challenged in the love department, however, the best thing we can do is to love those "love challengers", and especially love our children or enemies regardless. Love them through it, God does!

Sometimes we fail to love those who are closest to us. I know I do. How can this be? Whenever we discover ourselves falling short, forgetting to love, and/or uncomfortably less than "glorious", we can turn it around with a prayer to God to restore and fill our hearts. Seek His strength and love in union with His will. Where we are short, He is long.

Furthermore, we need not earn His love. God loves us so much that He simply loves on us when we are open to Him. In fact, He loves us regardless. Think of that verse 12 about *rewarding each person according to what he has done* as a bonus, like icing on the cake. His unconditional love is the cake; however, he dishes out rewards accordingly. Hmmm… According to what we have done. Does that inspire you to think about what you have done? How about that universal law of sowing and reaping? Has God, a family member, a friend, or your boss ever asked you to do something you did not want to do…but you knew you should? Like, forgive, serve, put forth your best effort even when you are tired, create, be kind to an unkind person, or even just be happy when things are going wrong? Mother Theresa would have said, "Do it ANYWAY"

This picture is posted in my office, in the front hall of my home, and the word and definition of "anyway" is printed and displayed on my bathroom counter as a reminder to just push through and do the right thing ANYWAY. I don't know about you, but I need a lot of reminders. Indeed, it can be hard but hang on to the following promise: **Those who sow with** *tears will reap with songs of joy. Psalm 126:5* Sign me up!

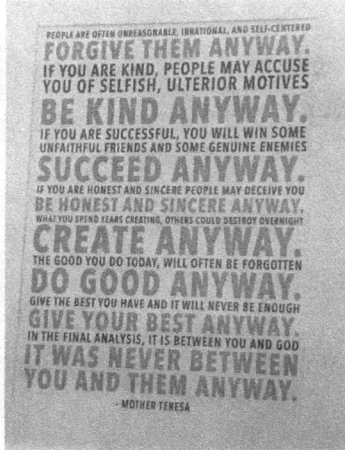 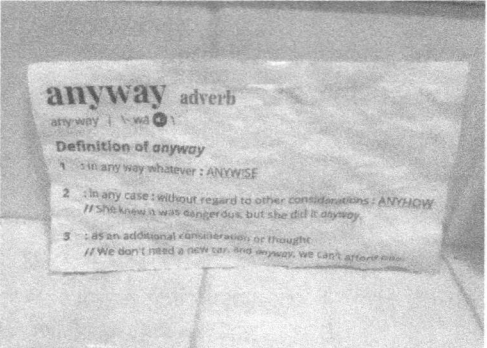

I have done good and bad things, which invoked *rewards* and *consequences*, but God never stopped loving me. This reminds me of the broken record phrase I repeat to my children, "Do you want *blessings* or *curses*? It's all about obedience, child!" When we see the manifestation of blessing and reward, it is all to God's GLORY! Just remember, he loves us no matter what. Regardless. That is another one of my favorite words along the lines of "anyway."

We are all God's children. He loves us, speaks to us, and he will reward us and make us strong if we will simply LISTEN. Look at the life of King David. He wrote, **"one thing God has spoken, two things I have heard"**. David was a good listener! He heard two things... that God is strong, and God is loving. To me, it seems like God's words multiply here. God's words can multiply as we share them, as we share His glory in our lives, and share our love in the lives of others. Just *listen, hear,* and *do* what God tells you!

I pray that God speaks to you today, that you will hear His words, be strengthened, and act upon them. May you find the love of God, allow it to take over, and activate in your life as you become able to love others as God loves you. Remember, God loves you wherever you are. When you are weak, He is strong. Glory!

Food for thought:
What area of your life do you need to strengthen?

Where would you like to see His glory?

IS IT SUNDAY?

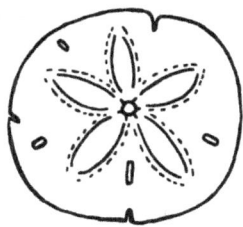

The alarm clock sounded this morning. I awoke, startled, bleary-eyed, rolling over to turn it off, with my first thought of the day, "Huh, isn't it Sunday?" Rewind a couple of hours... the dog woke me up to go out, and I noticed the alarm was not set so I flipped the switch on, then went back to bed. When the alarm startled me awake, I thought maybe it was Sunday, since the 5:30 a.m. alarm had not been activated the night before. To tell you the truth, I've done it the other way, on a Sunday at 5:30 a.m. the buzzer went off... and so did a rather annoyed husband!

In cheerful anticipation I still thought, "Oh yeah, it's Sunday!" As my brain began to download, I remembered going to church the day before. Ok, mystery solved, indeed, it is Monday. Then I thought how cool it would be if every day were Sunday. Get up, praise God, go to church, praise God, fellowship, get some rest, hang with the family. It must be like that in Heaven! Can it be like that here? I wonder, if you are a pastor, is every day like Sunday? Meaning, it's their job to do these things. How cool is that?

Well, how cool would it be if we did that, too, as we go about our day? Maybe that would be Heaven on earth. Wake up with

God in mind. Dress your best, even if it is work clothes. Just put forth some effort. It may pay off! **Eph. 5:19 speak to one another with psalms, hymns, and spiritual songs. Sing and make music in your heart to the Lord, always giving thanks to God the Father for everything, in the name of our Lord Jesus Christ.** I did not read anything in there about *only on Sunday!* Seems to me, this is like "whistle while you work" vs. grumbling and complaining. Do you ever catch yourself grumbling? I do. Ever had to put up with co-workers, friends, or family members grumbling and arguing? Hmmm... Let's look at **Phil. 2:13-14 for it is God who works in you to will and to act according to His good purpose. Do everything without complaining or arguing so that you may become blameless and pure, children of God.** I think this is beginning to sound more like a Sunday.

Ephesians 5:21 submit to one another out of reverence for Christ. Sounds like cooperation here. Wouldn't that make life easier? If everyone, or at least more people, cooperated with each other? In a perfect world. Now look at chapter six in **v.7 Serve wholeheartedly, as if you were serving the Lord, not men, because you know that the Lord will reward everyone for whatever good he does, whether he is slave or free.** That should make any job easier, doing it as unto the Lord in His service, not just "because" or for the paycheck. Years ago, my friend Donna shared that when she was upset with her husband, she would imagine she was serving Jesus, not the husband! This helped her keep a good attitude in times of adversity. I have referred to that scenario often over the years... probably not often enough!

What about when times get really tough? In Phil. 1, Paul answers this in **verse 18, *Yes, and I will continue to rejoice, for I know that through your prayers and the help given by the Spirit of Jesus Christ, what has happened to me will turn out for my deliverance. I eagerly expect and hope that I will in no way be ashamed but will have sufficient courage so that now as always*** (and not just on Sunday) ***Christ will be exalted in my body.*** Now those are some powerful words! I don't know about you, but when I am having a bad day, words like *eager, expect, hope, and courage* don't usually come to mind. But they need to. I need to. Oh, how they would help. If I carry words like this in my heart and soul, the likelihood of them becoming more of a default would increase. Think of eager expectation as jet packs to launch you up!

With courage, (and with God) we can eagerly expect a favorable outcome in which God will be glorified as we emerge stronger and victoriously through a difficult day or situation. This attitude rings power vs. helplessness. Imagine, pray, and meditate on positive outcomes. See it in your mind's eye, your heart, your soul, or whatever you want to call it but stop yourself from rehearsing negative outcomes, AKA WORRY. In practice as a psychophysiologist, I teach people to write positive affirmations to replace negative self-talk by speaking life into their world. Just like Sunday services offer a spiritual recharge, positive expectations and expressions of faith can make every day like Sunday.

We need not wait for Sunday. We do not need to be pastors to serve and encourage others. We can do it anyway (that favorite word again), any day. Maybe then our pastors would have a lighter load. For sure our loads would be lighter as we encourage ourselves and one another more frequently. It certainly helps to start each day by handing our concerns over to God and asking him to fill our minds, like spiritual breakfast. Every day.

Miracles come in cans, not in can'ts. -Joyce Meyer

Food for thought:
How do you feel about Sundays?

JAMES 1...THE FIRST SENTENCE

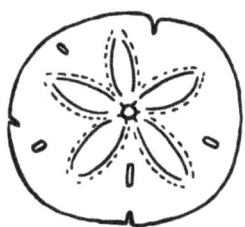

James 1:1 James, a servant of God and of the Lord Jesus Christ, to the twelve tribes scattered among the nations: Greetings.

In the first sentence of the first chapter of James, I noticed something for the first time today like never before, and I've read it many times. Am I a slow learner? James clearly identifies who he is... not as James the brother of Jesus, or James the professional whatever he was, but he defines himself as a SERVANT of God, and specifically the Lord Jesus Christ. Not just Jesus Christ, but the LORD Jesus Christ.

Here, James appears to be a man who knows WHO he is and who he is SERVING. To me, that's half the battle! It certainly helps to know who you are. Rick Warren wrote one of my favorite books on discovering your purpose. What an awesome tool that was for me when I was trying to figure out what to do with myself. At about chapter twelve I became the "Organic Produce Gal" and founded an organic produce co-op which later evolved into a farm stand and even a cooking show on local television. It all happened as a direct result of a prayer for purpose. God paved the way.

So, James stated who and what he was, a servant, then proceeded to deliver a message. He began with simple "Greetings." Notice to whom he sent the twelve greetings… not just to his buddies, not just to his church group, not just his family, or even his community. James sent twelve messages to twelve different tribes scattered among the nations. Remember, he accomplished this time-consuming task before postal service and email. Can you even imagine how that happened? Regardless, he sent his message to everyone who needed to hear it, never mind political correctness. Yeah, they had PC back then, it just was not called that yet. This great man did not hold back within his comfort zone of possible acceptance. He did it anyway.

James was a brave man with a mission and a message. Look out!

Food for thought:
What is your purpose or mission in life? (If you don't have it yet, read "A Purpose Driven Life" by Rick Warren)

Who are you serving?

JAMES VS. STORMY TRIALS

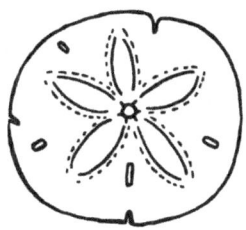

Now here is James the next act of bravery by James... in the second sentence he told his readers, **"Consider it pure joy, my brothers, whenever you face trials of many kinds"**

AAAHHHHH! What a paradigm shift! Joy? I usually perceive trials as negative experiences with varying degrees of angst, from minor annoyance to full blown torture. But joy? Not a working thought that typically occurs to me. How about you? Let's see how he explains himself...

"Because you know that the testing of your faith develops perseverance. Perseverance must finish its work so that you may be mature and complete, not lacking anything." Oh, I get it. James wrote this at a time when people were complaining, arguing, and living "worldly" despite their religious beliefs. This happens. To offer encouragement, he says to focus on perseverance, maturity, and fulfillment that come after this demand on faith. Hmmm... herein lies another opportunity for possibility thinking. A word comes to mind here. A word often heard, especially from my teenagers, "whatever." Perhaps these tests could be reframed with a *"whenever"* then focused accordingly, "James style", with a joyful outcome view. *Whenever* we face a trial, God has a purpose. It helps to look for the outcome or lesson. Usually, God is telling us to look at something beyond our current circumstances.

It can be difficult to see a purpose through all the fiery conflict. Typically, something like this will run through my head, "How can this be a godly thing when I'm in Hell's Kitchen?" Ah, just look out the window… I call this looking at the "lake view from hell's kitchen." Consider ***1 Cor. 3:12-15 If any man builds on this foundation using gold, silver, costly stones, wood, hay or straw, his work will be shown for what it is, because the Day will bring it to light. It will be revealed with fire, and the fire will test the quality of each man's work. If what he has built survives, he will receive his reward. If it is burned up, he will suffer loss; he himself will be saved, but only as one escaping through the flames.*** It looks here like God is at work within us. We will be tested and proven one way or another. We can be burned out, burned, or refined! When it gets hot, we can "open the window" and look beyond our circumstances. We can take this opportunity to look for our destination and prepare for arrival.

You might ask, "But how do I do it? I don't see it!" ***V.5 "If any of you lacks wisdom; he should ask God, who gives generously to all, without finding fault, and it will be given to him."*** God will show you, He can open the window, maybe even let out some heat! Just ask Him. Notice the part about "without finding fault." God refrains from judgment here, no qualifiers. Oh, I am so busted! Often, when people ask me for something (especially the kids) my brain fires up a list of terms and conditions. God gives generously to all, without finding fault. I think that's where forgiveness and grace come in to play.

V.6-7 "But when he asks, he must believe and not doubt, because he who doubts is like a wave of the sea, blown and tossed by the wind. That man should not think he will receive anything from the Lord; he is a double-minded man, unstable in all he does."

So, we must ask God with boldness and confidence, knowing he gives freely and generously. "Umm, well, uh, Lord, could you maybe blah, blah…" "No!" Or He may answer, "What? I can't hear you through all the doubt!" That sounds familiar to me, oops. He who doubts is like a wave of the sea, blown and tossed. I have felt blown and tossed around in wavy life storms, have you? Here James suggests that doubt is the root of the tossing and instability! Really? It seems so natural. The challenge is to replace stormy tossing with the stability of "no doubt wisdom prayer requests" to stand upon.

To conclude his epic view of stormy trials, James promises blessing. **V.12 "Blessed is the man who perseveres under trial, because when he has stood the test, he will receive the crown of life that God has promised to those who love him."** Now here, God does not give freely. The promise is for those who love him. **Deut. 5:33 Walk in all the ways that the Lord your God has commanded you, so that you may live and prosper and prolong your days in the land you will possess."** The promise is for those who walk in His ways.

Persevere "whenever", look out the window for God's purpose, love God, and be blessed. ***Is. 46:4 Even to your old age and gray hairs I am he, I am he who will sustain you. I have made you and I will carry you; I will sustain you and I will rescue you.***

Food for thought:
Describe your most recent trial or storm.

Looking back, what do you think was the purpose for this experience?

How did it or can it make you stronger?

IT'S TEMPTING

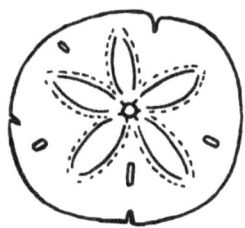

James 1:13 When tempted, no one should say, "God is tempting me."

Throughout the Bible, God never tempted anyone. Since the beginning, it was always Satan tempting people to sin by lying, deceiving, or provoking evil desires. "The devil made me do it!" That's right! ***"For God cannot be tempted by evil, nor does he tempt anyone;"*** Jesus was tempted by Satan for forty days, but he did not sin. He was successful in defeating the devil's antics. After forty days (or even a week) he must have been very weary. He certainly had an excuse but did not succumb. When Satan spoke tempting words, Jesus answered with the Word of God. Sin always contradicts God's Word, so when sin talks, always answer with the Truth. This is a great tactic to stay out of trouble. If and when you know what God says about a thing, you'll know what to do and how to get it right.

That is why it is so important to stay in the Word. I don't know about you, but I have a hard time remembering everything. Oh, in my pocket, I carry memory verses to program in my heart, but just don't always recall the numbers and exact words. But you know what? I get the idea! My heart knows the Truth. I can feel it in my soul. Did you ever catch yourself saying, "That doesn't sit right with me", or "I have a gut feeling", or "Ah, I resonate with that"? There's actually a whole physiology lesson here in heart rate variability coherence. It is when your brain, your heart, and your gut are in sync with each other through the vagal nerve and your autonomic nervous system (that part of your central nervous system like breathing that happens for the most part automatically) is balanced. Get it? Resonating on the Word is like a balanced diet for the heart, mind, and soul. How are we supposed to remember all that? A college professor once told me that you don't have to know everything, you just have to know where to look it up! All we need to do is search for the Truth. Whew! Amen.

There is this thing called a "concordance" in the appendix of most Bibles. There is even a whole huge concordance book… and the availability of internet searches. Like an index for the Bible, the concordance references every principle word or phrase in the scriptures and directs the reader to it. Consider it a Biblical Siri. Simply look up the word and it gives you a little snippet of how it was used in the sentence (for context) then follow along to the corresponding "address" or scripture reference. Browse through each verse pertaining to your subject matter then you can find an answer. So often it helps to "Look up, not down."

When facing temptation, recognize where you look. ***V.14 "But each one is tempted when, by his own evil desire, he is dragged away and enticed."*** It is not always the devil doing the tempting, rather our own evil desires pulling us away. Now, of course, not all desires are evil. It helps to stop and do a "safety check." Simply check the desire against God's Will or his Word. Remember the saying, "WWJD, or what would Jesus do?" Green light or red light? Better yet, "Is it a good light we can see and follow, or a dark idea pulling us down into a rabbit hole?"

"But I'm not Jesus! I'm not perfect, I'm only human!" Yes, indeed. ***1 Cor. 10-13 No temptation has seized you except what is common to man. And God is faithful; he will not let you be tempted beyond what you can bear.***" God knows we are only human. He lived as a human and even subjected himself to temptation, so he knows how it feels. You are not alone. You are just like every other human being who is being tempted daily. It will never go farther than that which you can bear. Just bear with it! Keep in mind all the promised benefits of walking with him, then ask yourself again, "Red light or green light"? It is important to answer the question before getting dragged off track by a desire fixed in your brain. It can happen at any moment, even catching you off guard, not fully recognizing the face of temptation. Satan wants to drag you away, out of God's will. He'll try really hard. Sometimes it is bad influence friends who try to drag you down. Put your boots on and get into warrior mode. Stand your ground.

1 Cor. 10:13b "But when you are tempted, he will also provide a way out so that you can stand up under it." Look around for an easy way out while standing your ground against that which attempts to pull you down! ***James 1:15 Then after evil desire has conceived, it gives birth to sin; and sin, when it is full-grown, gives birth to death."*** Avoid flirting with temptation. Speak to temptation with both the authority and the power to overcome it that comes from the Word of God, ***"for the wages of sin***

is death." Stand your ground and choose life that is never ending!

Food for thought:
Describe one of your temptations.

How did you handle it?

LEADERSHIP
Ref. 2 Chronicles 16-17

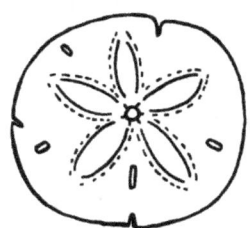

King Asa made a treaty with the king of Aram about relieving Judah from invasion by the Israelites. The seer Hanani busted Asa for relying on the king (a man) rather than on God. He reminded him of past victories in which mighty armies with great numbers of chariots and horsemen were simply delivered by God into his hand. God knew what Asa did. He witnessed this turn of faith from God to man. Let us tune in to the Word here for a moment... ***16:9-10 "For the eyes of the Lord range throughout the earth to strengthen those whose hearts are fully committed to him. You have done a foolish thing, and from now on you will be at war." Asa was angry with the seer because of this; he was so enraged that he put him in prison. At the same time Asa brutally oppressed some of the people.***

This looks like classic scapegoating at it's finest! Asa did not appreciate the seer's honesty in pointing out his mistake. A faithful leader would have heeded the words of a prophet who was doing his job by calling him out and holding him accountable. Politics. He could have chosen to do damage control and set things right, instead he had a tantrum, threw Hanani in prison, and took it out on his people. I'm thinking of the ripple effects citizens sometimes suffer through due to poor leadership. This can happen on the local level too, in churches, schools, and families. A leader must carefully consider decisions, advisors, and who protects them. Likewise, citizens should consider who they elect to govern them.

Three years later God literally took Asa's feet out from under him, plaguing him personally with a foot disease. Asa still did not seek help from the Lord, but from physicians. (v. 12-13) Now I do not see anything wrong with going to the doctor, but Asa neglected turning to the Lord for healing as well. This is a man who had seen God work in mighty, miraculous ways. At some point, he put his trust elsewhere. He didn't even have faith God would heal his feet. Twice, he consulted the wrong people. Go figure! He died.

Asa's son Jehoshaphat succeeded him as king of Judah. *2 Chron. 17:3-6: The Lord was with Jehoshaphat because in his early years he walked in the ways his father David had followed. He did not consult the Baals but sought the God of his father and followed his commands rather than the practices of Israel. The Lord established the kingdom under his control; and all Judah brought gifts to Jehoshaphat, so that he had great wealth and honor. His heart was devoted to the ways of the Lord; furthermore, he removed the high places and the Asherah poles from Judah.* Imagine that… Jehoshaphat gave it up to God and God gave it all to him. What a concept. He did not conspire to take it, nor is there any mention of him asking God to give it to him. Hmm… Now that is some powerful leadership. I think our country could use a leader like this!

Jehoshaphat's heart was devoted to God. He sent officials and priests to teach throughout Judah, taking with them the Book of the Law. Look what happened next in verse 10: **the fear of the Lord fell on all the kingdoms of the lands surrounding Judah** (I see rippling here), **so that they did not make war with Jehoshaphat.** The Philistines, perpetual nemesis, brought him gifts and flocks and herds of animals. Instead, they could have been raging in battle, held captive, or put to death (rewind a few chapters for a Philistine character profile). Jehoshaphat took up the "sword of the spirit" which is the Word of God (Eph. 6:17) instead of fighting with chariots and warriors. He did not *need* to fight.

Jehoshaphat became more powerful, collecting more wealth and servants, by making PEACE not war. He taught rather than fought. It seems the answer lies in teaching, not terrorizing. *Think of the applications…*

Jehoshaphat was a great leader, but now fast-forward to chapter 19. Like his dad, he also got a warning. Jehoshaphat had been helping the wicked and loving those who hate the Lord, two-timing so to speak. Jehu, the seer, warned him the wrath of the Lord was upon him. It did not matter that he set his heart on seeking God or that he rid the land of Asherah poles… he failed to give God 100% (buzzer noise). Unlike his dad, however, Jehoshaphat received and did not rebuke the warning given. Here's the first thing he did, **19:4 Jehoshaphat lived in Jerusalem, and he went out again among the people from Beersheba to the hill country of Ephraim** *and turned them back to the Lord, the God of their fathers.* He covered his territory, letting it be known they were to serve God alone.

Next, he appointed judges in each city. He gave them some serious guidelines to follow. *19:6-8 He told them, "Consider carefully what you do, because you are not judging for man but for the Lord, who is with you. Judge carefully, for with the Lord our God there is no injustice or partiality or bribery."* He appointed Levites in Jerusalem to administer God's laws and to settle disputes. Here's a summary of the orders he gave in verses 9-10: *"You must serve faithfully and wholeheartedly in the fear of the Lord. In every case that comes before you... no matter who or what the concern... you are to warn them not to sin against the Lord: otherwise his wrath will come on you and your brothers. Do this and you will not sin."* He concluded with this at the end of verse 11, *"Act with courage, and may the Lord be with those who do well."*

Jehoshaphat knew he needed godly people to administer godly justice in order to keep his kingdom aligned with, blessed, and protected by God. Wise man! In the proceeding chapters, readers of the Bible will see that God honored his commitment and leadership. God fought his battles and blessed his people as Jehoshaphat defended and honored his God.

Now here is a revelation: We can take advantage of each and every opportunity to administer justice at the local level, within our families and workplaces. Rather than groaning in complaint when forced to step in to settle conflicts as they arise, we can rejoice at these teachable moments. These are valuable moments that can be used to point out how we violate God when we violate one another. Family conflict offers a heaping portion of opportunity, especially as a parent. Sometimes conflict seems like the favorite sport of our children, they have so much time to practice! But we can change this by teaching them a new game, God's game. The playing field belongs to God. Children need to know that. Don't we all?

God has been taken out of public schools, government, and such. His Ways are being replaced with worldly ways. This has happened throughout history, just study the Old Testament, and look at what happened to these individuals over time. As the seers pointed out, when people violate God (foul), they score wrath! What a history lesson.

Oh, if I let these violations continue in my family, just like the kings of the Old Testament, I could be subject to wrath. This morning I asked God for a lesson. The children and the government have been on my mind. When I opened the Word, opened my HEART to the Word, God gave it to me. He is so faithful. His Word is powerful and timeless… or shall I say, *timely*? Imagine how many people may have consulted him this morning… yet He took the time to offer me a lesson on "never give up hope and leadership." God is such a loving, faithful father and leader. He is powerful and imparts his power to us, with us, and behind us as we follow him. We have the opportunity to follow his example, His Ways, and consider these history lessons as we lead our lives, our families, and our country. God is with us… or not, it depends on which way we go and whether we *take* him!

It is written that people perish for lack of knowledge. ***Psalm 82:5 They know not so they don't understand.*** This is like walking in darkness. If you find yourself walking in darkness, shine your light and the darkness goes away! In these stories, the seers shined their lights. Let your light shine as well. Don't let it go dark. Keep your pilot light on. Let God be your pilot.

Food for thought:
Are you registered to vote?

Describe a time a leader influenced you.

How did you respond?

PROVERBS 31:10-31
The Virtuous Woman

*(Embellished with Bec's modern-day translation/
version in parentheses.)*

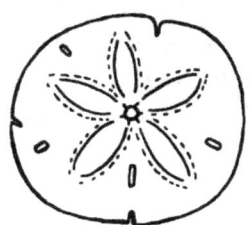

Times have changed considerably but virtue is timeless. Standards such as faith, charity, hope, fortitude, temperance, justice, and prudence reflect a person's character, worth, and confidence. They affect reputation and contribute to excellence and success on an individual and collective level. Moral standards are analogous to a measuring stick of integrity, intentions, values, and commitment but are sometimes cast aside in the wake of self-serving desires. **Ps. 37:4 Take delight in the Lord and he will give you the desires of your heart.** To me, this means, run desires through the God filter, focus on Him, and your efforts will bear fruit (or organic produce LOL).

10: She is worth far more than rubies.
(She is a priceless treasure, worth more than money, gold, credit cards, or fast cars.)

11: Her husband has full confidence in her and lacks nothing of value.

(Her husband trusts her, and she repays him many times with Good Stewardship over all his valuable household affairs. Nothing in this world can measure her value to him.)

12: She brings him good, not harm, all the days of her life.

(She brings him comfort and joy by restraining herself from upsetting him even when she is in the throes of hormonal fluctuations. She wishes him good, not harm, even when he leaves his clothes on the floor, or goes out with his buddies on her birthday. She knows God is not through with him yet, or herself for that matter!)

13: She selects wool and flax and works with eager hands.

(She selects fine materials, gym equipment, supplies, and works out with calloused hands.)

14: She is like merchant ships, bringing her food from afar.

(She shops online, brings organic crops from the produce district into the desert.)

15: She gets up while it is still dark: she provides food for her family and portions for her servant girls.

(She gets up at the crack of dawn, prays for her family, sees the kids off to school, and thanks God for her dishwasher and laundry room.)

16: She considers a field and buys it: out of her earnings, she plants a vineyard.
(She opened a farm stand to sell her organics to fellow "Produce Pals". She feeds her family well and her profits help support the family and her expensive horse habit.)

17: She sets about her work vigorously; her arms are strong for her tasks.
(She refers to her work as a lifelong "hamster wheel"; her arms are strong from shoveling horse poop every day.)

18: She sees that her trading is profitable, and her lamp does not go out at night.
(Trading her career for motherhood profits her family immediately and provides her a stockpile of treasures in Heaven. She continues working after darkness comes, and often falls asleep before the lights go off at the end of the day.)

19: In her hand she holds the distaff and grasps the spindle with her fingers.
(She brandishes a wooden spoon and grasps the keys to teenage son's truck.)

20: She opens her arms to the poor and extends her hands to the needy.
(She shares what God has given her and helps those who need to be lifted up. She knows that you can only keep what you are willing to give away.)

21: When it snows, she has no fear for her household; for all of them are clothed in scarlet.
(When monsoon season comes, she has no fear because her roof does not leak, and her home has air conditioning. When the sun comes out, her children and animals will dry and cover with sunscreen.)

22: She makes coverings for her bed; she is clothed in fine linen and purple.
(Not me, I learned how to make a cozy blanket by sewing a straight line but cried when attempting to crochet. Wearing mostly children's and workout clothes, my favorite color is chartreuse, and I have a passion for leopard prints. God help me!)

23: Her husband is respected at the city gate, where he takes his seat among the elders of the land.
(Her husband is loved and respected and taking his seat at the head of the family table and the "man cave" sound booth at church.)

24: She makes linen garments and sells them and supplies merchants with sashes.
(She creates healthy recipes, wrote a cookbook, sells organic produce, and distributes nutritional supplements and nontoxic cleaning products. She does her family a favor by taking them to the mall rather than making their clothes. She assembled a cool costume out of recycle trash for Earth Day one year.)

25: She is clothed with strength and dignity; she can laugh at the days to come.

(She carries herself with strength and walks with dignity. While embracing the dreams of her present and future, she knows both her husband and God are alongside. "Bolero the Magnificent" Tennessee Walking Horse carries her as well. She looks forward to a midlife crisis when she will tackle scrapbooking and drive a red car. She marvels at the thought of an empty nest.)

26: She speaks with wisdom, and faithful instruction is on her tongue.

(She assembles wisdom from her Bible and life experiences placing them into her spiritual nutrition book, which she uses to encourage her family and friends.

27: She watches over the affairs of her household and does not eat the bread of idleness.
(She keeps an eye on her family, watches what they eat, and never sits for long or else she will nod off and fall asleep!)

28-29: Her children arise and call her blessed; her husband also, and he praises her; "Many women do noble things, but you surpass them all."
(Her children wake up and ask her, "What are we going to do today?" They call her mean mommy… but her husband thanks her for taking such good care of the family and calls her the finest woman in all of Havasu. He knows that if it were not for all the salads and tofu cheesecake, he would not look so fine.)

30: Charm is deceptive, and beauty is fleeting; but a woman who fears the Lord is to be praised.
(Anyone can fake a good attitude merely to win approval. Youth and beauty are only skin deep and can be restored with plastic surgery, Preparation H, and wrinkle serum. A woman who can anchor her faith in God and weather the storms should be recognized… more than once a year.)

31: Give her the reward she has earned, and let her works bring her praise at the city gate.
(Give her a day off to shop with a Nordstrom Gift Card. Let her books and cooking shows be successful so everyone recognizes her name and the quality food and recipes she makes available to them. Word of mouth is always the best praise for any family business.)

"ED"itor's Cookie:

It helps to know you are not alone when attempting to be either a Virtuous Woman or a Virtuous Man who loves their God, their family, and their country. It is a narrow road to follow, not easy, because no one is perfect, but that's why we have Jesus. By being virtuous to each other, we can bring prayers, peace, patience, and perseverance, while taking up our Cross, following Him because we believe in His message.

Food for thought:
How does virtue apply to your life? Have some fun with it!

How do your actions influence others?

SONG OF A DESERT ROMANCE

Another "Becism" for fun, adapted from Songs of Solomon Chapter 2

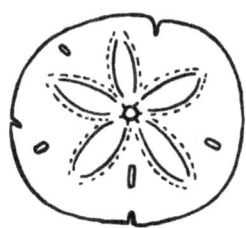

Beloved: I am a rose of Havasu, a cactus flower in the desert.

Lover: Like a wildflower among the scorpion weed is my wife among the "hoochie mamas."

Beloved: Like a citrus tree among the mesquite is my husband among the young men.
I delight to sit in the shade, his fruit is sweet to my taste.
He has taken me out for dinner. He loves me.
Strengthen me with oranges, refresh me with your juice, for I am weary, but I still love you.
His left arm holds my head up and his right arm begs me to stay awake.
Daughters of Arizona, I tell you, by the rabbits and coyotes of the plains:
Do not arouse or awaken love until the kids are in bed.

Listen! My lover! Look! Here comes his truck four-wheeling out of the desert, burning rubber up the street. My lover is like a racecar driver or a young bronco.

Look! There he stands behind our bedroom door, listening for a sign of life, he quietly peeks in. My husband said to me, "Wake up honey, I got a sitter, let's go out!" See! Monsoon season is over; the rain and winds are gone. The desert blooms: it's time to go camping, the cooing of quails is heard in the yard outside. The cactus sprouts prickly pears, and it is time to pull the weeds. Arise, come, my darling; you are still beautiful, we will pick them together.

Lover: My dove in the mounds of dirty clothes in the hiding place of your laundry room,

Show me your face,

Let me hear your voice; for it is muted by the churning of the washing machine.

Alas, your face will be restored when you peel off that clay mask.

Catch for us the children, the little varmints who tear up the house, make them clean their rooms!

I will do the dishes.

Beloved: My husband is mine and I am his.

He browses among the workforce until the sun sets and his job is done.

Turn, my lover, hurry home for dinner, and I will save something special for you later...

Food for thought:

Express some words devotion to your significant other or a loved one in a card or letter.

RECIPE FOR FRUIT

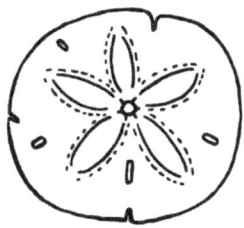

Do you ever feel ineffective or unproductive? I do. Some days I am on a roll. Things go my way, get accomplished, and work out in general. This is when life is good, I'm groovin', it is divine! On the other hand, there comes a day when it feels like I'm stuck in cement, running out of ideas, time, and energy. Frustration abounds. It does not feel good, not so groovy.

I found some encouragement, however, a recipe for spiritual nutrition in 2 Peter to satisfy my hunger for effective productivity. Check this out... ***2 Peter 1:3-9 His divine power has given us everything we need for life and godliness through our knowledge of him who called us by his own glory and goodness. Through these he has given us his very great and precious promises, so that through them you may participate in the divine nature and escape the corruption in the world caused by evil desires. For this very reason, make every effort to add to your faith goodness; and to goodness, knowledge; and to knowledge, self-control; and to self-control, perseverance; and to perseverance, godliness; and to godliness, brotherly kindness, and to brotherly kindness, love. For if you*** *possess these qualities in increasing measure, they will keep you from being ineffective and unproductive in your knowledge of our Lord Jesus Christ. But if anyone does not have them, he is nearsighted and blind, and has forgotten that he has been cleansed from his past sins.*

What Peter conveyed here, is that through God's divine power and our knowledge of him (we get that in the Word), we have everything we need to accomplish the glory and goodness he created us for. He reminds us to lean on God's promises to open the door of divine nature, escaping from a corrupt world caused by evil desires. Hmmm... could it be that when we come up short and frustrated it has something to do with our desires not lining up with God's recipe for quality? Did you ever make a mess in the kitchen, then clean up and start over? Likewise, we have that opportunity in forgiveness with God. Forgiveness and a measure of goodness, knowledge, self-control, perseverance, godliness, kindness, and love serve as a recipe to bear fruit; or field goggles to see. There's a heap of food for thought!

Perhaps the recipe for a glorious, good day starts with a helping of **faith**, faith in God's promises. Peter says add to that a measure of **goodness.** Next time you feel stuck, just move forward, and do something good. Take action to do even some little thing God would have you to do. I have found the best way to get my mind off my troubles is to do something to bless someone else. This almost always generates a warm, fuzzy feeling as it diverts focus from problems to blessing.

The next ingredient is a measure of **knowledge**. Think of those times and situations when you "don't know what to do." I remember as a young student, when I did not know or understand a word, my teacher or my mom would tell me, "Look it up!" I still have that big red dictionary full of words. Now I have my Bible, too, (actually, I had it then but I seldom referred to it) and the concordance tool that enables me to look up all kinds of situations, words, and find God's answers. For thousands of years, God's people had issues, conflict, and adversity. Many stories of triumph and defeat are documented. The common thread is that when believers looked at their situations, then looked obediently to God, they emerged victoriously. This offers us hope.

Next, Peter calls for the addition of self-control. Note there is no room in the pot for fear, selfishness, or doubt (bad flavor). These things are better left out or controlled. Sometimes you "gotta do what you gotta do." Just keep it together. God can help with that!

And never give up! The next ingredient is **perseverance**. Just like kneading bread or simmering a pot of spaghetti sauce, some things take consistency and time. I heard it said that God is a slow cooker in a microwave society. Most food tastes better after "stewing" rather than straight out of the microwave? Ok, well not popcorn, LOL. My husband always feels special when his dinner has been simmering for a while, baking in the oven, or even kept in the warming drawer ready for his meal. Even the house fills up with its aroma. I always feel sorry for my pets when I leave them alone with a crock pot full of yummy food they get to smell and salivate over all day long until we return for dinner. Likewise, God prepares us, he nourishes us, and He wants us to be ready in due time.

Add to perseverance, **godliness** (persevere in godly things) and to godliness, **brotherly kindness**. I grew up as an only child and gave birth to two sons a little over a year apart. I am no expert on "brotherly." Much to my dismay, these boys, while not Cain and Abel, they brawl! Oh, at times they collaborate, but even then, it is not always good. Often called to divide and conquer, I recall one peaceful morning when things were a little too quiet downstairs. I walked into the family room they had just decorated with bright red fabric paint. The boys got into my craft box and did a lot of unauthorized painting, including each other! Ironically, they had been wearing their matching white Vacation Bible School shirts (that now lie at rest in a storage box, waiting to be shared some day in the future). Another time, they helped each other get up into the pantry and refrigerator to pour chocolate chips and milk into bowls so they could eat it like cereal. Nice recipe! I can laugh about it now and will laugh again. Despite my upbringing and manic mommy parenting experiences, I have come to learn the meaning of brotherly kindness.

The final and most important ingredient is **love**. It all hangs on love. God tells us many times over to love one another as he loves us. In **1 Peter 4:8** Peter tells us, ***"Above all, love each other deeply, because love covers over a multitude of sins."*** Peter wrote these letters to encourage believers to stand firm in their faith despite false teaching and a society rampant with moral compromise. Where we have faith, hope, forgiveness, and love, there will be present an aroma of God's glory, most often accompanied by an effective, fruitful life.

1 Peter 2:10 Therefore, my brothers, be all the more eager to make your calling and election sure. For if you do these things, you will never fail, and you will receive a rich welcome into the eternal kingdom of our Lord and Savior Jesus Christ.

Food for thought:
Write a recipe for fruit in your life.

SCOOP OR POOP

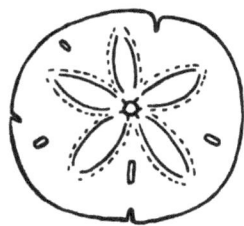

One morning upon beginning my routine four-mile run, I saw a big pile of dog poop, right on the path ahead. "Eeewww" I thought, "How disgusting and rude of someone to just leave it there. I always pick up after my dogs." As a pile of negative thoughts began to set in, it occurred to me this was setting myself up for a bad run. With an inspired train of thought, I began to ponder the whole dog poop placement thing… just bear with me for a minute while I clean it up for you.

Think about this amusing revelation… In life, some people are poopers, and some people are scoopers. Some people keep busy making messes, which in turn, forces other people to be busy cleaning up after them running damage control. For others, making the world a better place is their mission. Just like the mess I discovered on my run, whatever is left behind usually happens right in the path of the following person.

When comparing types of personalities, whether a small baby or a much older senior, age does not seem to make a difference when it comes to making and cleaning up messes. It seems that in general, people fall into one category or the other, yet have the potential to go either way. Messes affect the lives of young and old people, but in different ways that can elicit a negative or a positive response. It's all relative… age, actions, and environmental impact in the physical or spiritual realm. The point is we all share the same world, interact with one another, depend on each other, and have the option to choose our roles and experiences.

Seriously, if you think about it, some people just make a mess of things for others. The appearance of a beautiful time or place can change quickly when a real stinker comes along to influence the prevailing atmosphere. The "air" suddenly becomes a distraction of negativity. What people do may or may not be done intentionally, but their whole physical being compels them to do it anyway. The good news is we always have a choice to switch roles and deal with each "Character-Building Opportunity" as it occurs.

Why do you suppose there could be such negative stuff going on in our lives, our families, and our communities? Maybe it is related to what we take or let in and how we respond to material circumstances. In computer class, the instructor taught us "GIGO" or garbage in, garbage out. Likewise, the winning secret might come from a good attitude, good digestion, immune system maintenance, and good programming so that we will obtain a desirable outcome. Scoopers help to clean up the place while poopers provide a challenge! You know, we really could not have one without the other…

Regardless, every individual has the need to release negative things. However, we need to be careful where we deposit or leave it behind because there is always someone following in our footsteps. Jesus tells us to leave our problems at the cross so He can lighten our load of burdens. **Mat. 11:28 Come to**

me, all you who are weary and burdened, and I will give you rest. We all need rest and restoration. On the other hand, avoid letting a dung pile stop you in your tracks. Think of this as another character-building opportunity (CBO).

Poop on the path is not always as bad as it seems. God can use any circumstance for His good purposes. Without a messy CBO, perhaps we could miss a valuable lesson. These exercises or tests make us stronger and smarter! Sometimes they provide a blessing. One day I helped a friend sort through a pile of clutter in her garage, finding a *treasure* that was merely *junk* to her. To me, it was a blessing. On another level, consider what happens when a young girl makes a mess of her life with an unwanted pregnancy then decides to give up the baby to a loving home. The birth mother, new parents, and the adopted baby all receive an opportunity to find restoration and blessing.

There may come a time we need to let go of something in order to reach out for a future opportunity. Here is what Paul had to say about moving forward in his letter to the Philippians: ***Phil. 3:13-14 Brothers, I do not consider myself yet to have taken hold of it. But one thing I do: Forgetting what is behind and straining toward what is ahead, I press on toward the goal to win the prize for which God has called me heavenward in Christ Jesus.***

Deut. 28:12 The Lord will open the heavens, the storehouse of his bounty, to send rain on your land in season and to bless all the work of your hands.

2 Chron. 15:7 But as for you, be strong and do not give up, for your work will be rewarded. When we experience character-building opportunities and accept them, there is a potential to receive a blessing, which makes us stronger. Just keep the difficult moments in context and maintain a good attitude about them. Why? Take a look at the following scriptures: *Eph. 6:7-8 Serve wholeheartedly, as if you were serving the Lord, not men, because you know that the Lord will reward everyone for whatever good he does, whether slave or free.*

Phil. 2:14 Do everything without complaining or arguing. 1 Peter 4:11b If anyone serves, he should do it with the strength God provides, so that in all things God may be praised through Jesus Christ. God uses both poopers and scoopers to make the world a better place according to His plan. Rewards are promised when we choose to follow His path.

Scoop or poop? Every day brings opportunities to give and receive, to serve or be served. Likewise, life challenges are for givers and receivers. How will you choose to act when the opportunity presents itself? My choice of words used in this Chapter is distasteful, but they do bring home the point that everything in life is not always sweet like honey. We have choices. How we choose does make a difference to others, the world we live in, and to God.

When we give it up and serve Him, He, in return, gives to us. He will give us what we need, the right heart and spirit to get the job done. *Ez. 36:26 I will give you a new heart and put a new spirit in you; I will remove from you*

your heart of stone and give you a heart of flesh.
It does not matter who we *are*, who we *were*, or from *where* we come. What matters is what we do with the opportunities at hand and how we choose to approach them. God will give us the tools and the knowledge to use them according to our individual talents.

Eph. 4:21-24 Surely you heard of him and were taught in him in accordance with the truth that is in Jesus. You were taught, with regard to your former way of life, to put off your old self, which is being corrupted by deceitful desires; to be made new in the attitude of your minds; and to put on the new self, created to be like God in true righteousness and holiness.

2 Cor. 5:17 Therefore, if anyone is in Christ, he is a new creation; the old is gone, the new has come!
Whether a pooper or the scooper, with God's help, you can do His will while serving Him. Poop or scoop? The choice is yours!

Food for thought:
What part of your life will become - - - a legacy left behind?

Will your life have an impact on those who follow in your footsteps?

For what purpose did God make you?

Have you ever failed to act on a situation?

HUMBLE PIE

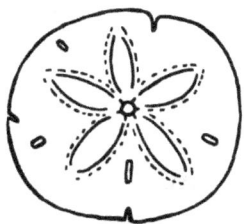

Recently, someone served me up a heap of humility. Not sure whether it was truly in order, I turned to God for His "Humble Pie" recipe and "nutrition facts." The Bible has a storehouse of wisdom about humility. This piece is my report back to you after a long journey through the humble aisle in His market. Did you ever eat humble pie? Yeah, it is good for you and tastes just fine when you serve it to yourself but when someone else dishes it out, humble pie loses its flavor. The virtue of humility is a gift from God and has many lessons to teach us as it stirs up some Holy Spirit wind and then the debris settles for collection in the aftermath. With each twister, we know that we remain covered by God's radar of Love. He sets the table and maps the storm. It is up to us to digest and navigate! Every virtue has its roots deeply embedded in humility. The process of learning begins by baring ourselves before the Lord. Trouble comes when you do not eat your share of the pie, pretending the rules of life do not apply to you specifically, but are meant for others. We are all worthy and loved by God and we all need a plate of spiritual nutrition from time to time.

Let us "read the label" taking a closer look at this compilation of "nutrition" in humble pie… then in the next chapter we'll focus on the recipe and how to eat it!

Prov. 11:2 When pride comes, then comes disgrace, but with HUMILITY comes WISDOM. Who wants to be foolish? I want to be smart! With humility comes wisdom. ***Ps. 25:9 He guides the HUMBLE in what is right and teaches them his way.*** The Bible says we can turn to God for guidance, but one must have a dose of humility to go there. In order to learn, one must one must have an open mind and be willing to consider the lessons of a teacher, the experience of an elder, or the wisdom of a wise man instead of playing the "wise guy" know-it-all. It is not enough just to submit humbly to God, we must be respectful of all opinions and learn from each other. With every slice of humble pie comes a lesson. Our attitude depends on whether we focus on the *learning* or the pie server!

Sometimes humility comes in the form of an apology. Sometimes the lesson is that we need to make a situation right, turn it around, or take it back. It takes humility to admit when you make a mistake, rather than covering it up to save face. The only thing saved by cover-up is the ego, but not really, because ego is usually the problem with pie in the face. A humble apology can develop character out of ego. Apology improves rather than saves face. Perhaps a little pie in the face when needed is good for our countenance once cleaned up… makes your face shine!

Titus 3:1-2 Remind the people to be subject to rulers and authorities, to be obedient, to be ready to do whatever is good, to slander no one, to be peaceable and considerate, and to show true HUMILITY toward all men.

Phil. 2:3 Do nothing out of selfish ambition or vain conceit, but in HUMILITY consider others better than yourselves. Wisdom begins when we start by putting ourselves aside, hearing and listening to those who know better and to God! Once again, when that slice of pie comes to your table, don't just send it back… don't look at the server, just know where it came from and take a taste. See what it can do for you and clean off your plate. Invite God to help with the digestive process.

When seeking GUIDANCE, we must first LISTEN for directions, which come when we HEAR the words. Oh, it also helps to ask for directions when lost. That is a humility thing! A lot of folks turn to God only when they are lost, but then complain that they do not hear Him. Throughout history people have had issues with the humility it takes to admit when help is needed, to ask and listen for directions. Here's what one group did… ***2 Kings 22:19 Because your heart was responsive, and you HUMBLED yourself before the Lord when you heard what I have spoken… I have HEARD you, declares the Lord.*** They listened to the Lord when He spoke against them. He heard and sent them in the right direction once they turned in humility. Sometimes we need to close a door or take a turn to get on the track God has for us. It takes humility to set aside our own directions or destinations. It takes humility to accept that God knows best, but He will take us where we need to go. That's an example of humble pie nutrition!

Sometimes we need not only wisdom and guidance, but DELIVERANCE from troubled times. Look at what God did in the second book of Chronicles to help his people. ***7:14 If my*** *people, who are called by my name, will HUMBLE themselves and pray and seek my face and turn from their wicked ways, then I will hear from heaven and will forgive their sin and will heal their land.*

12:7 When the Lord saw that they HUMBLED THEMSELVES, this word of the Lord came to Shemaiah: "Since they have humbled themselves, I will not destroy them but will soon give them deliverance.

12:12 Because Rehoboam HUMBLED HIMSELF, the Lord's anger turned from him, and he was not totally destroyed.

33:12 In his distress, he sought favor of the Lord his God and HUMBLED HIMSELF greatly before the God of his fathers.

Four times in one book we see that humility resulted in deliverance, forgiveness, and a second chance. Holding on to pride means your hands carry the seeds of your own destruction. When in the throes of distress (or how about even when you just begin to feel it coming on?), turn to God humbly rather than asking questions like "What are you doing?" or "Why me?" Simply ask Him what he wants from you and "What are you telling me?" It may be an apology, a turn, a lesson, or closing a door. Be Humble, hear the answer, and then follow God's will for you. God can fight our battle or put us in our place, it depends on the pie. When my slice of pie was delivered, the first thing I did was to question the server, wanting to send it back! Then I ate the pie, asking God to deliver me to my place.

God will shelter, save, and sustain us if we invite him to join us on *the* journey of understanding that sometimes we do not get our way. Sometimes we are better off to humbly submit to His will or way.

Zep. 2:3 Seek the Lord, all you humble of the land, you who do what he commands. Seek righteousness, seek HUMILITY; perhaps you will be SHELTERED on the day of the Lord's anger.

Psalm 18:27 You SAVE the HUMBLE but bring low those whose eyes are haughty.

2 Sam. 22:28 You SAVE the HUMBLE, but your eyes are on the haughty to bring them low.

Psalm 147:6 The Lord SUSTAINS the HUMBLE but casts the wicked to the ground.

How does He do it? I think it has something to do with an all knowing, understanding, and forgiving God giving us grace. *Prov. 3:34 He mocks proud mockers but gives GRACE to the HUMBLE.*

1 Peter 5:5b God opposes the proud but gives GRACE to the HUMBLE.

Hmmm… humility must be important because it is mentioned so many times in the Bible. Could it be one of the buttons on the elevator to Heaven? There are enough people in this world who try to bring us down. I want to remain in God's graces, lifting me up!

We invite trouble when we attempt to lift OURSELVES up. You cannot do it on your own for long because your ego takes over and pulls you down to lower and lower levels. The key to keeping up lies in humility. Sure, you can climb up the corporate ladder and with enough strength, you can climb a rope, but it is a lot easier to take the elevator. Just push the humility button and step in.

Mat. 23:12 For whoever exalts himself will be humbled, and whoever humbles himself will be exalted. Hmmm… according to this verse, it looks like the God elevator lands at the top, but the climber may take a fall.

Prov. 15:33 The fear of the Lord teaches a man wisdom, and HUMILITY comes before HONOR.

James 4:10 HUMBLE yourselves before the Lord and He will LIFT YOU up.

Usually we must wait patiently on the bottom floor for our directions. Sometimes we even stop on a floor to let others join us. However, God always arranges the details for a safe arrival when we follow His will, riding on His "elevator".

1 Peter 5:6 HUMBLE yourselves, therefore, under God's mighty hand, that he may lift you up in due time. God is the timekeeper who determines what happens to us and when. The lifting is God's part. Waiting humbly is our part.

Prov. 25:6-7 Do not exalt yourself in the king's presence, and do not claim a place among great

men; *It is better for him to say to you, "Come up here," than for him to HUMILIATE you before a nobleman.*

That sounds like humble pie a la mode! Let God be your elevator, it will taste better.

Sam. 2:7 The Lord sends poverty and wealth; he HUMBLES and exalts.

Prov. 22:4 HUMILITY and the fear of the Lord bring wealth and honor and life. God can will us to be rich or poor depending upon what He has planned for us. He can take us down or lift us up. It all depends upon how we accept the pie. God is in charge, He is just, and He might even test us to see what pie we will choose or that which we serve. ***Deut. 8:2 Remember how the Lord your God led you all the way in the desert these forty years, to HUMBLE you and to test you so that in the end it will go well with you.*** Don't we all want things to go well for us? ***Psalm 149:4 For the Lord takes delight in his people; he crowns the HUMBLE with salvation.*** He's even got us covered in salvation...that is, if we eat humble pie.

Don't just eat it, wear it! ***Col. 3:12 Therefore, as God's chosen people, holy and dearly loved, clothe yourselves with compassion, kindness, HUMILITY, gentleness, and patience. 1 Peter 5:5b All of you, clothe yourselves with HUMILITY toward one another.*** God says to clothe yourself in humility. Wear it with pride like your favorite team jersey. Be on God's team. Let humility be your label. Finally, when you win, give God the glory. ***Is. 2:11 The*** *eyes of the arrogant man will be humbled, and the pride of men brought low; the Lord alone will be exalted in that day. Is. 66:2 "Has not my hand made all these things, and so they came into being?" declares the Lord. "This is the one I esteem, he who is humble and contrite in spirit, and trembles at my word."* When the time comes, give God the glory, you did not do it by yourself.

Ah, humble pie can be good or not, it depends who does the serving. This is one case where serving yourself before others is best. It has no calories but offers benefits that stretch far beyond nutrition. Consider it spiritual nutrition that will make you strong and take you far and above a little Twinkie. Amen.

Food for thought:

Describe a time you ate "humble pie." Did you serve it to yourself or was it given to you?

How did it turn out?

HUMBLE PIE, PART II...THE NEXT STEP

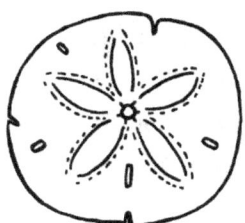

Now that we know the facts about humble pie, let's talk about the recipe and how to eat it. As with any other nutritious food like broccoli, just because we know what a benefit it is, does not necessarily lead us to cook it up or eat it. So, here is a little recipe and some serving tips…

What are the key ingredients of humble pie? Start with the crust…

Usually when making a pie, you start by spraying or coating the pan with a material to keep it from sticking. In this case, we want the opposite. We want it to stick…well to US anyway! So, let us pray that God will "spray us" with a Holy Spirit coating of stuff to help us "stick" to the task at hand and that we will retain the lesson in humility. Next, we lay the foundation or "crust." The foundation is God's Word. Whenever we want to make something good, it helps to have good instructions. When we want spiritual "food" we have learned to look to God. So, line the pan with a crispy crust of Godly wisdom on humility (as learned from the last chapter).

Next comes the pie filling. There are many types of pie. I'm thinking in addition to fruit pies, we have cream pies and even potpies and meat pies. Let's just stay away from mud pie! Humble pie could be filled with lots of stuff, whip up some cream out of spiritual "milk", add a little "fruit" of the spirit, then cover it in prayer with a top layer of crust. You could also fill it with spiritual meat for a main course, sprinkled with a dash of "salt." Savory or sweet, it's all good when filled with high quality, godly ingredients.

Sometimes we just mess up the recipe and it does not turn out right. We may need to add or delete an ingredient or two. We might have to start over again. Some ingredients complement each other and some just do not mix. Ask God to help you with the recipe. You may even ask another experienced, successful "cook" for assistance. This is an act of humility!

Any good pie will need time to set. Some pies are chilled, so we either chill out or we may choose to bake the pie. It may require some heat and time to cook. It is according to God's time. He sets the timer. We must listen for the ding and take it out of the cooler or the oven when it's ready. Once again, to submit to timing other than our own is an act of humility.

Chow time! Can you smell it? Many people smell their food before they eat it. That is a good idea... sniff it out, make sure it smells good and right. Sometimes you cannot tell what kind of pie it is until you smell, taste, or look at it. So, check it out first! Now get a knife and plate. Cut a slice and put it on your plate. Pray a blessing over it. God promises humble pie will deliver blessing. Pray you will receive it! Receiving humble pie as opposed to whatever else we may want to consume is yet another example of humility.

Psalm 34:8 Taste and see that the Lord is good. Take a taste. Did you ever try something and not like it, then develop a taste for it? Chew on it for a while. Swallow it. Let it digest, absorbing into every cell of your body and soul. Ask God to show you what it is doing or will do for you. Watch what happens. Be nourished and receive the blessing. You might even want another helping. You might want to share.

Food for thought:
Describe your piece of pie. What was in it?

Did it taste good at first?

How did it nourish you?

SPOOKY

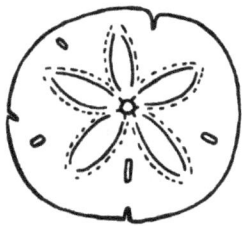

I love horses. God says where our treasure is our heart lies. In this case, I'm busted! Years ago, there was a treasure trove one block down the street from my house. A tack shed full of gear (with crosses inside and out), two paddocks for two horses, and a giant mesquite tree with singing birds that covered our space in shade. It was not all about the horses. I discovered right away that when working with animals many times your size, weighing in at 800-1500lbs, one needs a storehouse of prayer! That is why "Tack Shed Ministries" evolved. Within that old shed were my favorite Bible, a tattered volume that saw me through raising my three children through their preschool and elementary years. While I interact with a newer, working model now, I hang on to the old one. It stood by on the shelf alongside a box of tissue, ready for action when any nearby cowboy (or "wanna-be" cowgirl such as me) needed a Word. Oh, horse lovers need a Word all right. Here is a testimony for you...

One summer I had the bright idea that my daughter and I could have a lot of fun riding our horses as "Fighting Knights" mascots during football games on the home field. We rode successfully in a parade, now this would offer us a challenge and an opportunity to muster up high school spirit. After discussing it with the school administration and signing our lives away on the liability release, we got to work preparing our steeds. The first step involved desensitizing them to objects or situations that might "spook" or startle them.

Sometimes horses startle or even freak out at unfamiliar objects or noises. It can become frightening and dangerous in an instant. They can get hurt or hurt others on the scene if they rear up, kick, buck, or run out of control. Conjuring up an array of "spooky" scenarios to familiarize them with anything that might startle them, I exposed them to shiny objects, flying balls, horns, drums, balloons, took them out in the blustery wind, walked them by blowing tarps and bags, and rode them during a loud thunder storm. We crackled plastic water bottles, aluminum cans, and even littered their stalls with this kind of trash so they would step on it, "crunch!" The last test before entering the field would be the flags. At this point, I had a revelation.

Patiently working with the horses, I trained them not to freak out at unfamiliar sights and sounds. This made us safer and able to ride with pleasure. Animal instincts tell them to be guarded and watchful. They are "prey" animals who despite their size and strength, must flee from predators in the wild. For them, it is a survival thing that happens whenever they perceive a threat. Horses usually settle down once they figure it out. Assured they need not "freak out" at every little thing that comes along their path, my horses have learned to trust me not to endanger them. Comforted by my reassuring voice of love, they do not even need to *move*. It helps when they hear this voice, but **I** must remain calm for them, too. Then it dawned on me... (Here's the revelation part) GOD DOES THIS WITH US!

Ps. 16:8 I have set the Lord always before me. Because he is at my right hand, I will not be shaken. Just as I am at the side of my horse to steady him, God is at my side to steady me. He is at your side as well. ***Is. 41:13 For I am the Lord your God, who takes hold of your right hand and says to you, do not fear; I will help you.***

God loves us. He loves to spend time with us. He patiently works with us, exposing us to "spooky" things, knowing they cause no harm. Like animal instincts found in horses, He wants us not to react in an unnecessary or dangerous manner. He sends things our way to test us, too. Everybody's spooky things are different, but likewise, they are harmless distractions we perceive as threatening. However, God is in control and he does not want us to get hurt or even fear harm. During a big storm, Jesus said to his disciples, ***Mark. 4:40 "Why are you so afraid? Do you still have no faith?"***

Like the horses and disciples, we can attend to our master's (God) voice over the distraction, remaining calm and unmoved, averting potential harm. The key lies in our focus and the state of our spirit. Paul pointed this out in ***2 Tim 1:7 For God has not given us a spirit of fear, but of power and of love and of a sound mind. (NKJV)*** It's the reactive freaking out that can get us in trouble. There are neurophysiological underpinnings to all of this. Fear results in a primal limbic lobe hijack over the sound part of the mind which is cognitive executive function. We need a balance of power here to keep things in check. Oh, sometimes I still get scared and freak out! Try this one if you cannot hear his voice when you get spooked, ***Ps. 66:8-10 Praise our God, O peoples*** (vs. crying out in fear) ***let the sound of praise be heard;***

he has preserved our lives and kept our feet from slipping (Whatever does not kill you makes you stronger) ***For you, O God, tested us; you refined us like silver.*** Sometimes I think to myself, "I'll be a shining star when this is over!" ***Ps. 108:1 My heart is steadfast, O God; I will sing and make music with all my soul.***

Be steady. Whoa there, easy does it! Keep breathing. ***Pr. 29:25 Fear of a man will prove to be a snare, but whoever trusts in the Lord is kept safe.*** Trust God to talk to you and listen to His voice above all others. Ride on His wings through the spooky times. You will become a strong and Mighty Knight.

Food for thought:
What "spooks" you?

Write a prayer asking God to guide you through these experiences.

TESTING, TESTING

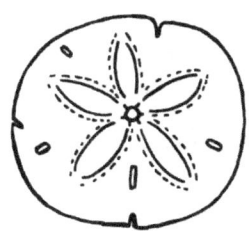

Genesis 22:1-2 Some time later God tested Abraham. He said to him, "Abraham! "Here I am," he replied. Then God said, "Take your son, your only son, Isaac, whom you love, and go to the region of Moriah. Sacrifice him there as a burnt offering on one of the mountains I will tell you about." God called to Abraham. "Here I am," Abraham replied. God told him to sacrifice his one and only son. No comment here from Abraham. Speaking from my point of view, certainly I would have been loaded with questions. Perhaps what we call sacrifice, he called worship.

V. 3a Early the next morning Abraham got up and saddled his donkey. He took with him two of his servants and his son Isaac. He got up *early* the *next* morning without question or hesitation. ***V.3b When he had cut enough wood for the burnt offering, he set out for the place God told him about.*** He was seriously obedient. He got the wood. Can you see yourself doing that? Honestly, I probably would have just showed up to ask questions like, "Hey God, are you serious? After all we went through and how long we waited, you REALLY want me to KILL him?" As if on autopilot, he did what he was told. Yep, God was his pilot, let's see what happened next…

V.4-5 On the third day Abraham looked up and saw the place in the distance. Can you imagine what might be going through his mind for three days? **He said to his servants, "Stay here with the donkey while I and the boy go over there. We will worship and then we will come back to you."** He told the servants to stay with the donkey while he goes "over there" to worship with the boy (he did not divulge the plan to sacrifice his boy to anyone, duh!). Furthermore, he proclaimed, "**WE** will come back to you." as if he knew in advance God did not *really* intend for him to go through with this plan. Did he *know* it was a test?

V.6-8 Abraham took the wood for the burnt offering and placed it on his son Isaac, and he himself carried the fire and the knife. As the two of them went on together, Isaac spoke up and said to his father Abraham, (Now, he is confused!) **"Father?" "Yes, my son?" Abraham replied. "The fire and the wood are here," Isaac said, "but where is the lamb for the burnt offering? Abraham answered, "God himself will provide the lamb for the burnt offering, my son." And the two of them went on together.** When Isaac asked where the lamb was, Abraham promptly answered with confidence, "God himself will provide the lamb for the burnt offering, my son." He *did* know it was a test! He knew God would provide, that's how he was able to do follow such incongruous instructions. Oh, there's more to it! First, he built an altar there.

V.9 When they reached the place God told him about, Abraham built an altar there and arranged the wood on it. Ever notice how whenever Abraham goes somewhere or has an issue to contend with, he builds an altar right where he is, and he prays to the Lord? Hmmm... he stops to worship and seek God. ***V.10 He bound his son Isaac and laid him on the altar, on top of the wood. Then he reached out his hand and took the knife to slay his son.*** How far do you suppose you would go before you hold back? Abraham was willing to go all the way, he went forward almost to the point of death... then, aha! He heard a voice, an angel of the Lord from heaven. He knew that voice. ***V. 11-12 But the angel of the Lord called out to him from heaven, "Abraham! Abraham!" "Here I am," he replied. "Do not lay a hand on that boy," he said. "Do not do anything to him. Now I know that you fear God, because you have not withheld from me your son, your only son."*** Like a sheep listens to its shepherd, he listened to that familiar voice on a regular basis. He let that voice guide him wherever he went. Can you imagine the outcome if Abraham had been so preoccupied with his own grumbling, complaining, doubting, and worrying that maybe he would not have *heard* that voice over his own? Sometimes we miss things because of aimless or harmful distractions. Abraham heard the word that provided his son's deliverance.

God's is a safe voice, and if familiar, like the sheep, you will be able to distinguish and follow it above all others. I don't know about you, but often I hear that "still small voice" and still question it. I question myself. I do not always listen the first time. Oh, that sounds familiar. Thinking of how "apples don't fall too far from trees". I'm thinking of my children. My apples, AKA fruit.

Abraham saved the life of his boy by listening to that voice before it was too late. Not only did he listen, but he also responded, "Here I am." That's twice in one chapter. He not only paid attention, but he offered himself, his whole self, and his son. His response was timely, with no hesitation. Not "Oh, just a minute, I'm in the middle of something..." He did not listen with one ear while his cell phone or his friends talked in the other. Had he not listened attentively; he could have missed that voice with disastrous outcome. The angel confirmed Abraham's fear and trust of God when he did not withhold.

V.13-14 Abraham looked up and there in a thicket he saw a ram caught by its horns. He went over and took the ram and sacrificed it as a burnt offering instead of his son. So Abraham called that place The Lord Will Provide. And to this day it is said, "On the mountain of the Lord it will be provided." He found a ram after claiming the Lord would provide. He did not pass it off as a coincidence, either. When you walk in God's will, he provides a way. **Lev. 26:3 If you follow my decrees and are careful to obey my commands, I will send you rain in its season, and the ground will yield its crops and the trees of the field their fruit.**

Amen! But it gets even better. The angel is going to speak again, **V. 15 The angel of the Lord called to Abraham from heaven a second time and said, "I swear by myself, declares the Lord, that because you have done this and have not withheld your son, your**

only son, I will surely bless you and make your descendants as numerous as the stars in the sky and as the sand on the seashore. Your descendants will take possession of the cities of their enemies, and through your offspring all nations on earth will be blessed, because you have obeyed me." Finally, this was Abraham's dream! He obediently offered what God wanted him to sacrifice and he received much more than he bargained for. In fact, he set the stage for his future descendants and their descendants. He sowed a precious seed and reaped a nation. Oh, how I long to prepare my children for the future. How I long for blessing in my family.

Such "stories" or events show us that in order to receive provision, we must LISTEN and FOLLOW THROUGH with what God calls us to do, without hesitation. If we remain faithfully in covenant with the Lord, we will be blessed. If our children follow along with us obediently, they too, like Isaac, will receive the blessing.

He may call us to do something that seems to hurt someone, like our children, but he would never put them in harm's way. He is only trying to bring us to the place he wants us to be. Just remember, be careful WHO you listen to! Ah, blessing, sign me up!

Oh Lord, forgive me for all the questioning, doubt, and hesitations. I pray that I will always hear your voice, that my family will hear your voice, and see your glory through my actions, confident attitude, and faith. Thank you for speaking to me today.

Food for thought:
Describe a time when God "tested" you.

How did you respond?

WHEN GOOD THINGS HAPPEN TO BAD PEOPLE

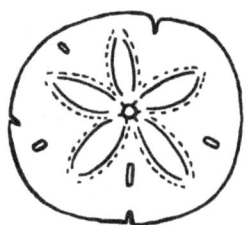

Let me just preface this chapter briefly by letting you know that at this time, I am in the throes of an angst-fest. My spirit is off, my heart aches, longing for comfort, and my feelings are not good. My aim is to restore the balance, get closer to God, farther from my drama, and show you how it gets done. So, come along with me, I promise the outcome will be good. With God, it always is...

Years ago Rabbi Harold S. Kushner wrote a book called *"When Bad Things Happen to Good People"* to help his readers through the grieving process, shedding light on how God works in our lives through both good and bad experiences. As he was interviewed before millions of viewers on the Phil Donahue Show, he offered eloquent, compassionate words of comfort, filled with the love of God. Inspiration settled in my heart as I watched this man who overcame incredible grief use his own tragic experience to bless others. "Take that, Devil!"

Now here I sit, with a GREEN (as in jealousy) coffee cup in hand. I choose a cup each morning to reflect or encourage my mood when "going to coffee" with God. What a poor choice today. Despite recognizing my feelings, I continued down that jealous path, busted! Ok, it is never too late to repent and fix it. This one goes to the dishwasher. How appropriate, wash the cup and cleanse the attitude!

Despite having addressed that business, the situation remains at heart. Teach me, Lord! What about when good things happen to bad people? Despite all the time spent reading about how God blesses us when we do the right thing, walk in His ways, and take the narrow road and all that, every so often I witness some bad person basking in the blessing as well. Now for the confession…it makes me mad. "No fair!" I say to myself, with expletives racing through my heart and soul.

Lesson One: Don't be the judge. Let God be the judge.

The first thing going on here is judgment. I'm judging these other people. ***Mat. 7:1 "Do not judge, or you too will be judged. For in the same way you judge others, you will be judges, and with the measure you use, it will be measured to you***. Ok, this must be given up. God, it's not up to me, you are the judge, you have better qualifications and know the truth anyway. One day I will be on the hot seat and want proper judgment!

The next part of that chapter in Matthew says to ask, seek, and knock. ***"Ask and it will be given to you; seek and you will find; knock and the door will be opened to you. For everyone who asks receives; he who seeks, finds; and to him who knocks, the door will be opened."*** This is a promise, so claim it! Ask, seek, and pound on God's door for help to see it through His eyes. "Lord please shed your light and judgment on the truth, I resign!"

Lesson two: Don't compare blessings.

I switched out the coffee cup and started over. This one says MOM on it and has pictures of all the things a mom does. With a lot to do and a family to focus on there is no time to waste thinking about what someone else is doing. I resigned from that position. It's hard enough to keep up with my own family. Most of us have enough jobs and plenty of blessings to be thankful for but get out of the thankful mode when we look at someone else's life. Most of the time I'm happy for and inspired by a great story of people's blessings and success. I was ok watching that program and became inspired by Harold Kushner. Other times, however, upon looking at someone's success (like today), I react quite differently, with anger, jealousy, and confusion. It was that good people, bad people judging thing that threw me for a loop. It happened during the comparison, U-turn!

Gal. 6:4 Each one should test his own actions. Then he can take pride in himself, without comparing himself to somebody else, for each one should carry his own load." We need to dwell in our own accomplishments and blessings, without comparing. Everything is relative. We can compare ourselves in many ways to many others, but that does not mean we should. Paul also points out that each one has his own load. The load we carry is unique and affects our actions and accomplishments, making them look different when taken into consideration. Just look at the Special Olympics for example.

Now just play algebra and plug different variables into the problem to come up with the right answer. Look at your own page, use your own numbers, and stand on God's promise to solve the mystery variable revealing the answer to the original question about why good things happen, to whoever they may. Remember ask, seek, knock.

God, I pray in advance for the truth and answers you promise to reveal. I pray for patience as I wait on you and for the peace that surpasses all understanding. May I see as you see, hear as you hear, and love as you love. Amen.

Food for thought:
Describe a time you may have judged or compared yourself to others.

Thank God for your gifts and for creating an incredibly special YOU!

ARE YOU READY FOR CHRISTMAS?

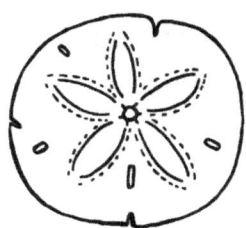

A neighbor asked me, "Are you ready for Christmas?" Ahhhh! My face flashed with "reindeer in the headlights" alarm. Then I thought, "Do I have to be?" It was only December 8th for crying out loud! I did not respond to her query. Keeping the thought to myself, engaging that "in your head voice" mode so as not to offend anyone. I took some time to process my feelings on the matter. "Not even close", I finally answered, following an unusually long pause for such a simple question.

Warning (shameless self-disclosure here- being transparent and honest): I struggle with Christmas. The reason for sharing is for the potential to resonate with any readers who may feel similar. This chapter of my soul may encourage likeminded individuals to redeem the holiday for themselves as well. If you are one who thrives on the typical plethora of holiday traditions and expectations, perhaps you will pray for me! If not, be forewarned. Go on to the next chapter, Happy New Year!

To me, it was not so simple. Every year I dread the hoopla added to my already busy schedule. For instance, I feel pressure to take the perfect family picture. It's stressful, my family is not perfect, and it seems dishonest (while a nice idea) trying to make us look like it for the sake of a photo. Three bickering kids, two big dogs, one boa constrictor, *and a partridge in a pear tree! (Add a little music note graphic here)* I'm supposed to be spreading holiday cheer, not headaches! In utter frustration, one year I gave up trying to capture the perfect photo, instead, sharing the candid shot taken of my children the day I caught them in the bathroom decorating each other with gooey purple toy slime. It was a classic happy photo of them cooperating in a group effort to have some fun. Everybody loved it! Well, except for a certain group of three slimy little elves. The following year they agreed to dress up and pose for that perfect Christmas photo, no drama!

Add the holiday baking. All year long I try hard to keep the family healthy, stay in shape, and limit our sugar intake. Now the rules change… and I'm supposed to feel good? And riding the blood sugar roller coaster is supposed to HELP celebrate the season? Not here.

Add the decorating. I do not like clutter. It makes me uncomfortable and means more stuff to clean. I enjoy a few carefully placed decorations and rotate a few meaningful items here and there throughout the year. Some remain always, like the ceramic nativity scene that adorns my fireplace mantel. I cannot bear to box it up, preferring to celebrate the gift of Jesus every day! Don't forget the pretty lights. I like them on and try to shine my own "light" as much as possible. My husband's nickname (among others) is "Mr. Kilowatt." He's into conserving energy. We have timers now. Sometimes I time out, too.

Add the holiday gatherings. How about those family affairs? How about when your family has some dysfunction? It seems to stand out and become more painful during the holiday season. I love and appreciate my immediate family and friends every day, but there is an empty spot because it's Christmas and my traditional family tree was chopped down. Well thankfully, God gave us our own family and fellowship, so be it!

Add the shopping for gifts. I learned by watching my mother-in-law, God bless her, that when you see something special you think would bless someone you know, just buy it, or make it if and when you can. Save the gift for an occasion (even if it is not until Christmas) or just whenever. Do not wait until once a year. Often, I don't know what someone would want, except for the kids, they usually make it clear!

Did I leave anything out? Probably. You know what is out at this point?

My "LIGHT." **Ps. 27:1 The Lord is my light and my salvation – whom shall I fear?**

Mat. 5:14-16 You are the light of the world. A city on a hill cannot be hidden. Neither do people light a lamp and put it under a bowl. Instead they put it on its stand, and it gives light to everyone in the house. In the same way, let your light shine before men, that they may see your good deeds and praise your father in heaven.

John 8:12 "I am the light of the world. Whoever follows me will never walk in darkness but have the light of life."

I'm concluding that perhaps holiday stress dims my "light" and the way to turn it back on is to focus on He who is the TRUE source of my inner light. Maybe if I stop worrying about all those outward things and just be transparent (I think I just was), that "light" will shine like a lamp as I walk in it. This way, perhaps others will see the reflection or light of Jesus that comes out of my heart. This sounds like a gift of its own, compared to the grief I cause my family and friends in the mire of stress and depression as the "holiday humbug girl" everyone wants to hide from!

I cannot make the perfect Christmas, but God knew how to do it. *2 Cor. 4:6 For God, who said, "Let the light shine out of darkness," made his light shine in our hearts to give us the light of the knowledge of the glory of God in the face of Christ.*

1 John 1:7 But if we walk in the light, as he is in the light, we have fellowship with one another, and the blood of Jesus, his son, purifies us from all sin.

Now here is the ultimate gift... *Acts 4:23 For the wages of sin is death, but the GIFT OF GOD is eternal life in Christ Jesus our Lord.*

Regardless, of all those holiday traditions, here is my take on the whole thing...

I believe every day is a gift. Years ago, I worked with a doctor who often said, "Every day is Christmas!" I liked that. We can bless people and celebrate the gift of Jesus every day. Some people only do it once a year because they feel an obligation. How special. Well, it's the *thought* that counts. Some people don't even *have* the thought. Some people don't know how to *express* the thought. Some people get *offended* at the thought. Some people, like me, feel like they cannot get it right no matter how hard they try. God loves us anyway, every day. Rewind. If we lived every day like it was Christmas, we would always be ready. We would receive a blessing every day, especially as we bless others and recognize the blessings in our own lives. **2 Cor. 9:15 Thanks be to God for his indescribable gift.**

Have you received the gift of Jesus? Is the gift of Jesus the same as Christmas? It depends. Traditionally, at least what I was taught, Christmas is a time of year when we, as Christians, celebrate and honor the birth of Jesus Christ. God sent Jesus, his son, to redeem us from our sins and give believers the gift of eternal life in Heaven with him. We celebrate the day he was born, his birthday. Well, we celebrate for an entire season. Why is that? When did that start? It started with the birth of Jesus and ends with our eternal salvation. What about all the fanfare in between? It seems to start earlier every year as people prepare for "Christmas" or the "holidays." Does it take so much time and effort because this birthday celebration is so important? I wonder, but not really, not most of the time anyway.

These days we tread on thin ice when we publicly acknowledge the reason for celebration of our holiday, our Holy day, the birth of Jesus. Yes, there are other beliefs and other religious holy days. None seem to stir up as much recognition and hoopla as Christmas. Hmmmm… Does importance have anything to do with that? Now I wonder. Some people have no beliefs, yet they celebrate the holiday. Do you wonder about that stuff, too? I asked an atheist about it once. "Don't want to talk about it" was the reply. Does not want to talk about it, but will celebrate, nonetheless. Hmmm…

Well this holiday is ours and I don't want to "sugar coat" it for the sake of political correctness and don't feel the need to coat it with sugar and wrapping and bows and plastic to make it sweeter than it already is to me! If the focus is on a gift TO Jesus FOR His Birthday, then the most appropriate blessing would be the gift of our own hearts to Him and the sharing of the greatest gift of all which is HIS gift. The message of salvation, which includes forgiveness and love, IS his gift because what he really wants is for US to be with HIM. Ah ha, it's really about fellowship, fellowship in the family of believers. It's beginning to feel like I fit in now. Here's a cool thing, for this particular birthday celebration, everybody gets the gift. No one is left out unless they choose to be left behind.

Food for thought:
Have you received the gift of Jesus?

What do you do to prepare for Christmas?

HAPPY NEW YEAR!

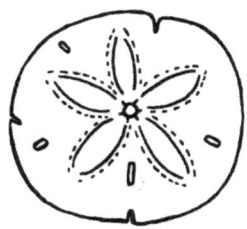

Christmas is over and now we are focused on the New Year. We looked at images of a Baby Jesus for a season, now we see the image of a Baby New Year. When Jesus was born, we got a New Testament. How cool is that? We have a whole book of forgiveness and testimony. Now that's a tool to take into the New Year with us.

I keep hearing people say, "Thank God this year is over!" Yes, it's been a tough year economically. I won't argue that, but it could have been worse. For a lot of people, it *was* worse, for some, it was better. I have two thoughts on the matter... and I'm going to reach into that New Testament "toolbox" and get to work on them.

Here is my first thought: we should not take the good things for granted.

Heb. 12:28 Therefore, since we are receiving a kingdom that cannot be shaken, let us be thankful, and so worship God acceptably with reverence and awe (even when Christmas is over). As Christians, we received the gifts of Christ, forgiveness, and salvation, amen! If all else fails, we still have something to be thankful for. I bet there are other things. It helps me to turn our focus toward what we have from what we do not.

A second thought is we can make plans to do whatever is in our power to improve what might be missing or needs to be fixed in our lives. We can ask God to help with that as well, He has a lot more power than we do! **Phil. 4:6 Do not be anxious about anything, but in everything, by prayer and petition, with thanksgiving** (oh, there's that word/tool again) **present your requests to God.** One of my favorite tools/verses is this one: **Mat. 7:7-8 "Ask and it will be given to you; seek and you will find; knock and the door will be opened to you. For everyone who asks receives; he who seeks, finds; and to him who knocks, the door will be opened.** It comforts me to know that God wants to listen and help. We are not alone on this.

So, beginning with a heart of thanksgiving, moving on to some improvement in life… but do we really need to wait for an official day like Thanksgiving or January 1 to do it? I don't think so. We can start off each day with a thankful prayer and look to step forward in a positive direction with something that needs work in our lives. Every year we have a Jan. 1, New Year, but every DAY is a new day. **Lam. 3:22-23 Because of the Lord's great love, we are not consumed, for his compassions never fail. They are new every morning; great is your faithfulness. Ps. 188:24 This is the day the Lord has made; let us rejoice and be glad in it.** Just like with a year, sometimes I'm really glad a day is done, and I get to start over the next morning! God is faithful and I can be, too. God is compassionate and never fails to love us each and every day. Sometimes we fail though. Setbacks happen, guaranteed. But our God is a God of second chances (and third and…). The beauty is, we can start over, any time. I prefer to start in the morning.

I looked up the word *morning* in my big exhaustive concordance to find a scripture reference. There were almost two pages of references, just for the one word! God spoke a lot of words about *morning*. Busy time. God spoke in the morning; listeners woke up and saw His manifestations in the morning; folks rose up in the morning, and God rose in the morning. Things came to pass, appeared, disappeared, and flourished in the morning. Folks made offerings, executed judgments, directed prayers, sowed, reaped, sang, and even roosters crow in the morning.

"Well," you might say, "I'm not a morning person." Just get up and get going or get over it! Years ago, I made it a habit to wake up before anyone else in my home. That was tough duty when my children were young. It was always worth it though, when I made the effort to check in with God and my cup of coffee before all the day's mayhem overtook my schedule. Experts say that breakfast is the most important meal of the day, not to skip it. To me, this devotion time is the "Breakfast of Champions" **for we are more than conquerors through him who loved us. Rom. 8:37.** God speaks to me (or maybe it's just that I hear him better) when it is quiet, and I am still. **Ps. 46:10 Be still and know that I am God.** We often hear about taking a *stand*, but we also need to be *still* at times and listen for God. He honors that commitment made to give him the first part of my day. It helps me focus and stay on track.

Well isn't that what most of us talk about doing come January? Get on track, focus on a goal, or change something? Maybe it would be easier if we got to bed earlier? Sometimes what you do the day or night before has everything to do with how you are when you wake up in the morning! Maybe that's what this change thing is all about. Let us sow good seeds for the New Year, each day. Let us tend to our lives as we would tend to a field or nurture a young baby, with gentleness, love, and compassion. Most of all, let us be thankful and glad for a new day, a New Testament, and a testimony! And don't forget your "toolbox."

Food for thought:
How do you usually start your day?

What was your resolution this year?

PEACE OUT

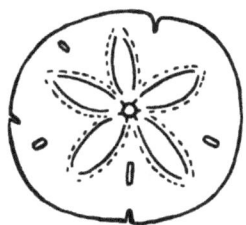

Oh, help me Lord! Another "Character-Building Opportunity" (CBO) day lurks in my midst today. Why doesn't more peace exist in my home instead of stormy upheavals? In the Bible, James declares that storms make us strong when we persevere. Perhaps God wants to strengthen me in an area with this new CBO. It's going to require a heaping measure of strength and character to get through this one. Like any other storm, there's usually a lesson attached. Ok, Lord, help me look for what I can learn from this as we tune in to the "weather report."

Stormy conditions at the Bassham house! When calling to check and see if my daughter was at her girlfriend's house, I discovered my fourteen-year-old girl (emphasis on the 14 here), was instead, out with a sixteen-year-old boy. Busted! She was not where she was supposed to be. Sparing you the drama that followed, let's skip to the thankful part. ***Hebrews 12:28 Therefore, since we are receiving a kingdom that cannot be shaken, let us be THANKFUL, and so worship God acceptably with reverence and awe.*** I want to be strong, not shaken, so my focus will shift to thanksgiving. Things can always be worse. Experience has shown me that it always helps to look at what to be thankful for instead of grumbling about something, especially a CBO.

Here's my thankful part... Thank you God, for the "mommy radar" that prompted me to call the Mom of my daughter's friend. Thank you to my friend, for some helpful information. Thank you, Gram Messer, Christian musician, for the beautiful music. Your "Out of Ruin" CD provided just what I needed to hear while driving around in fear and anger. God helped me stay on the right road (in more ways than one). Thank you to my son, for finding your sister and bringing her home safely. Whew! The weather cleared up some, but now what about the fallout? How does a Mom orchestrate damage control after such a storm?

Help me, Lord! I'm crying out to you, again! "Hello, are you listening to me???" **James 3:17-18 But the wisdom that comes from heaven is first of all pure; then peace loving, considerate, submissive, full of mercy and good fruit, impartial and sincere. Peacemakers who sow in peace raise a harvest of righteousness.** I knew to look up (to God, to His Word) rather than become downcast with negative thoughts this morning while looking up "peace". My spirit longs for peace; a state of tranquility, freedom from disturbance, freedom from disquieting or oppressive thoughts and emotions, harmony in personal relations, and agreement to end hostilities between those in a state of enmity. Peace! It was not enough to just read about peace, a certain Mommy (who would be me) needs to mellow out and learn how to swallow whatever it takes to bring more peace into her home. **Psalm 85:10 Love and faithfulness meet together; RIGHTEOUSNESS and PEACE kiss each other.** Apparently, righteousness and peace go together. Perhaps the absence of peace is rooted in the lack of righteousness. **Ps. 85:13 Righteousness goes before him and prepares the way for his steps.**

Putting it all together, one might conclude that peacemakers sowing in peace can grow a harvest of righteousness that will last a lifetime. Yeah, righteousness is preferable to anarchy, conflict, and guilt, isn't it? Sign me up! This sounds like peace versus a storm. But what is righteousness? Would that make me pompous and full of myself, like the Pharisees?

Webster's Dictionary describes righteous as meaning acting according to divine or moral law, free from guilt or sin. In my words, it means doing the right thing for the right reason. Now remember, we do not have to be perfect, because that's where forgiveness comes in. The peacemaker must sow with the proper attitude, right? Sow in peace. But I'm angry, hurt, offended, betrayed… oops, I have a lot of "weed seeds" in my heart today! Can you hear me God? "Put the bag away, Bec, throw away the weed seeds! Dispose of them cautiously, "hazmat" style so no one will get hurt." God directs us to be Peacemakers. Sow in Peace, then with God's help we can raise a harvest of righteousness.

Fruit of the spirit seeds can be found in **Galatians 5:22-23, But the fruit of the Spirit is love, joy, peace, patience, kindness, goodness, faithfulness, gentleness and self-control.** Oh, fill my seed bag, Lord! When my daughter needs to remember something important, she writes it on her hand. **Faithfulness** and **self-control** were not written on her hand last night! Oh, I'm seeing a teachable lesson here, perhaps a purpose in the storm. We'll explore writing and sowing today, sowing Galatians 5:22-23 seeds to reap the fruit of the spirit!

The law of sowing and reaping says that we reap what we sow. So, if we sow fruit of the spirit seeds in peace, we will come home to a harvest of righteousness. In a perfect world. It is not always perfect though, but to me, life in the Spirit looks better than life out there in a world of anger, conflict, guilt, and strife. Life begins with seeds. Ok, with the Word of God and with help from Holy Spirit, we can sow the seeds we want to grow. We can sow these seeds into our lives. We can sow them into our children and family. We can sow them into our worldly society so people can see growth in the spirit.

After sowing the seeds, we must become "gardeners". Every garden requires some tending in order to grow abundantly. Here's where we get to work. The gardener makes sure there is adequate sunshine and water. God provides us with all the necessary ingredients for a bountiful harvest. He gives us sun and rain. He also gave us His Son and the love of the Holy Spirit to rain down and help us grow. We will need to add some prayers to nurture our garden and follow the garden path of righteousness in our lives. **Mat. 5:45 He causes his sun to rise on the evil and the good, and he sends rain on the righteous and the unrighteous.** Fertilize your life with "soul food" to provide the best nutrition for growing in your love of God. Also, remember that both seeds and life begin small, growing little by little each day until harvest time.

With such optimal great farming conditions, expect to see some weeds grow because God allows rain to fall upon the righteous and the unrighteous. Weeds will choke out and absorb life from our planted crops, so we must remove them. In fact, Biblical references tell us to burn away the chaff! It's easier to remove weeds when they are small. It's also easy just to chop them down, but weeds must be removed from their roots or they will grow back. Even once removed, new weed seeds sprout, therefore weed control must continue on a regular basis.

After a certain period, our good seeds will produce a harvest. Remember that seeds and life begin small, growing little by little each day. Remember God always has His perfect timing, which is where patience plays a role as one of those fruitful seeds we planted. Every day is a good day for planting and tending, but God prepares us for *harvest* according to His timing. ***Gal. 6:9* Let us not become weary in doing good, for at the proper time we will reap a harvest if we do not give up.**

How can a parent deal with a "stormy" child? How can anyone deal with any stormy person? The ANSWER is to approach the storm in peace. ***Eph. 4:31-32*** Get **rid of all bitterness, rage and anger, brawling and slander, along with every form of malice. Be kind and compassionate to one another, forgiving each other, just as in Christ God forgave you. Eph. 5:2 live a life of love, just as Christ loved us and gave himself up for us as a fragrant offering and sacrifice to God.** We can sacrifice our stormy reactions simply by sowing both peace and love. Liken the CBO tribulations to tilling and look to the harvest as reward for a job well done.

***Rom. 5:1-5* Therefore, since we have been justified through faith, we have peace with God through our Lord Jesus Christ, through whom we have**

gained access by faith into this grace in which we now stand. And we rejoice in our sufferings (storms), *because we know that suffering produces perseverance; perseverance, character; and character, hope. And hope does not disappoint us, because God has poured out his love into our hearts by the Holy Spirit, whom he has given us.* The answers come from turning to God and His words as written in the scriptures. Follow this formula and Love will pour into us from the Holy Spirit. We are God's children, the fruit of His "garden." He supplies our needs and prepares us for harvest time.

Lord, please bless the little garden you gave to me so that it may be fruitful. Bless it to abundance that we can share and provide for others as well. Thank you for your Son, seeds to plant, sunlight for growing, rain to quench thirsty roots, your Holy Spirit, and the fertilizer of Your Word. I pray in the name of Jesus for help with weed control and for a bountiful harvest in this season and many seasons to come. Amen. Now with confidence I shall go forth in peace and give meaning to the words---

---Peace Out!

Food for thought:
Think back to one of your "stormy" days.

Write down the issue facing you at the time.

List the negatives (weed seeds) as well as the positive (good seeds)

What did you learn from the experience that can be sown into the next generation?

MARCHING ORDERS

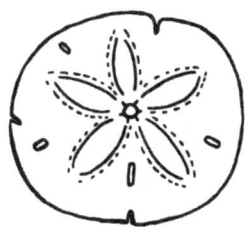

Through his angels, God gave John a series of revelations to show his servants what must take place in the future. In chapters 1-3, God dished out a series of warnings, or "marching orders" to the angels for the seven churches in the province of Asia. The first thing that occurred to me was, "What about everyone else?" Guess I'll figure that one out later, but for now, let's check out these warnings...

To the church in **Ephesus**:
Despite everything else they did right... hard work, perseverance, intolerance of wicked men, testing false apostles, and endurance... they fell short on LOVE.

> *Rev. 2:4 "You have forsaken your first love. Remember the height from which you have fallen! Repent and do the things you did at first."*

The Church started with love. A lot of things changed since then. We still need love. Even the Beatles sang, "All you need is love." Every commandment hangs on love. Our reward is the right to eat from the tree of life.

To the church in **Smyrna:**
No rebuke for the Smyrnaeans, only a warning that some of them are about to suffer for ten days (they may be tested, imprisoned, and/or persecuted... even to the point of death, for up to ten days). **Rev. 2:10b "Be faithful, even to the point of death, and I will give you the crown of life."** So, these guys were doing it right, they had it going on. God was pleased with them, yet they will suffer. It seems unfair. Well look at the reward. Suffer for ten days and receive the crown of life, eternally. Ok, got it.

To the church in **Pergamum:**
They remain true to their faith and the name of God; however, some church members were following false teachings. God called upon them to repent.

Rev. 2:16 Repent therefore! Otherwise, I will soon come to you and will fight against them with the sword of my mouth." Well we know God's Word is a sharp sword. Let us take it up in battle. God fights for us. In this chapter, He calls the people of Pergamum to fight for the truth of His teaching. Here's the reward: **v.17 "I will give some of the hidden manna.** (Isn't that the same food God provided for the Israelites when they were starving in the desert long ago, but then they complained about it after a while? Maybe they were starving like the Israelites.) **I will also give him a white stone with a new name written on it, known only to him who receives it."**

Hmmm... a white stone with a new name. What does that mean? I'm confused, but I know God has all these things figured out. Just remain faithful, ask God for wisdom and clarity. He will reveal it in time. His time.

To the church in **Thyatira:**
God acknowledges their deeds, love and faith, service and perseverance, and their increased productivity. Nevertheless… oh, that word gets to me, even though I use it often! As if it does not matter about the big picture, it always comes down to one more thing…

> *Rev. 2:20 Nevertheless, I have this against you: You tolerate that woman Jezebel…"*

God's beef here is about them tolerating and following a woman who is a false prophet leading people astray into immorality. He tells those who do not follow her to hold on to what they have until he comes to take care of it. It might be best to stay out of the way! The reward: **v.26 "to him who overcomes and does my will to the end, I will give authority over the nations."** In verse 28 he also gives to the obedient the "bright and morning star." Upon reading Revelations to the end, it is revealed this star is Jesus.

To the church in **Sardis:**
He describes their reputation as being alive, but dead. He calls upon them to wake up, strengthen what remains, complete their deeds, remember what they have received and heard, as well as obey and repent. Whew! That's a long list! He likens them to those who wear soiled clothing while he refers to followers who walk in His ways as worthy, dressed in white: **Rev. 3:5 "He who overcomes will, like them, be dressed in white.**

I will never blot out his name from the book of life but will acknowledge his name before my father and his angels.

To the church in **Philadelphia:**
Rev. 3:7 These are the words of him who is holy and true, who holds the key of David. What he opens no one can shut, and what he shuts no one can open. Here, God explains that he alone holds the key to David (Heaven). Only He determines what is open or shut. This looks like an "open and shut" case. The Philadelphians kept his Word, kept his command to endure patiently, and did not deny God's name. Therefore, he plans to keep them from the hour of trial and testing that is to come upon the whole world. *V.9 I will make those who are of the synagogue of Satan, who claim to be Jews though they are not, but are liars – I will make them come and fall down at your feet and acknowledge that I have loved you.* Here, it looks like He will make the hypocritical Jews (not all of them, but the hypocritical ones) fall at their feet and acknowledge God's love for his believers. He tells his followers to hold on to what they have, and he will make them pillars in His temple. The door opens. Then he will shut the door, so they never have to leave this place. The angel is going to get a new name now, too, and this city of God will be called the New Jerusalem.

To the church in **Laodicia:**
Rev. 3:19-21 "Those whom I love I rebuke and discipline. So be earnest, and repent. Here I am! I stand at the door and knock. If anyone hears my voice and opens the door, I will come in and eat

with him, and he with me. To him who overcomes, I will give the right to sit with me on my throne, just as I overcame and sat down with my Father on his throne.

Laodiceans receive rebuke for being neither cold nor hot, but lukewarm. This is so distasteful to God that he is going to spit them out! Sounds like if you're not on fire, he's going to put you out! The Laodiceans *say* they have acquired all they need, but Jesus describes them as wretched, pitiful, poor, blind, and naked. He counsels them to put salve on their eyes so they can see as he sees them.

Oh, how I long to see as God sees so I can get it right! Here is that door thing again. It seems to me, that in life, we are guaranteed to struggle. Struggle is analogous to the door. When you see the door, or crash into it, ask God for help. Knock on that door, go through the struggle (aka the "door") WITH HIM, then you'll arrive just where God wants you to BE… and that is WITH HIM, ALWAYS.

Food for thought:
What are your "marching orders?"

IT'S YOUR TURN

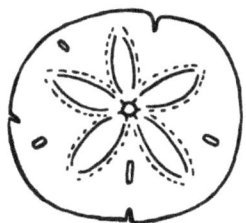

Now it is your turn! After reading with me for 21 days, begin by asking God to give YOU a Word. Open the Bible to whatever page He may lead you toward. Read a chapter, then ask yourself the following questions:

Which verse stood out to you the most? Write it here.

What is God telling me?

How will you apply the verse to your daily life?

It's your turn! I encourage you to do this for "breakfast" (or whatever time you like to feed your soul) each day. Eat the "spiritual breakfast of champions!" See how you grow stronger and closer to the Lord as you conquer any CBO's that blow into your life.

Begin with your own blank journal as I did years ago.

You don't have to be a writer to keep a journal, just answer the questions. You may even have questions of your own.

Nutrition For Your Soul

It is also a good idea to record your prayers and the answers He provides. It will be your own "nutrition book" treasure box collection of stories, wisdom, and lessons learned.

There are no wrong answers with God. He is the teacher.

Ask Him to fill your pages, to fill your life.

Bless you!

ACKNOWLEDGMENTS

This book was created with a passion and thirst for God's guidance and direction. Many thanks to my family, husband Ty, sons Ryan and Aaron, and daughter Cheyanne, for giving me the reason why. To my parents who brought me into this world and took me to church when I was a kid; especially to my mother who, as an elementary school teacher, instilled within me a passion for reading and writing. To Cathy Geringer for being my cheerleader and a best friend all these years, for your confidence and belief in my abilities whenever I expressed doubts.

Thank you Hardy and Jeannie Edmonson for being my Cowboy Dad and Spiritual Mom; for being there through all the laughter and tears, and for loving our family for who we were, just like your own. Your support was my "Jesus with skin on" and I do not think I would have survived without you as my neighbors. Your cowboy and spiritual wisdom have been priceless.

To Durmond Blatnick, Pete Brown, and KNLB Christian Radio for your prayerful support and encouragement to be present in the moment, to serve faithfully where I was called in the process of becoming the person God wanted me to be …patiently, as I waited to figure out where that may eventually lead according to His will and timing.

Nutrition For Your Soul

Thank you to The Organic Produce Gals, the "Flying J's" Jeannine, Joli, Jonnie, Jennifer, to Robin, Lynn, Missy, and Kat who served, along with all the "Produce Pals" who supported and participated in the Organic Produce Gals co-op and Foothills Farmstand ministries. This and your fellowship was a direct answer to my prayers for refuge, fellowship, nutrition, and entertainment from fruits and vegetables, nuts, health, the pumpkin fest, hula hooping with Amanda, and even playing the "what won't Daisy (my chocolate lab) eat" game. All organically grown. You surrounded me with love, laughter, and prayers. Many of you were test readers for these chapters, hot off the press, and encouraged me to compile them for this book. You will never be forgotten.

To the Carradine family for fostering my horses and my heart during a time of financial and spiritual upheaval.

To Deb and James Whitney and Pure Sports Recovery for offering me a venue to heal and serve at the same time, thus the fulfillment of my dreams to connect the dots between mind, body. And soul. For that epic introduction to Dr. Joseph Maroon. Thanks to you, Joe, for encouraging me and all the readers of your book Square One to develop a healthy, balanced life when the spiritual and relationship sides of my life were nil as I suffered on a line going nowhere.

To Kana Nootenboom and the Aoki family for your prayerful support, confidence, and yet another opportunity to serve, grow, and love. For reminding me to seek God in everything, to sit with Him, and trust Him to provide. To Steve for inspiring me to be a DJ; a DJ of the brain, to sing and dance and inspire others to bask in the rhythm of heart and soul.

To all the "Character-Building Opportunities" for the experience to learn, grow, and develop. Once again, with utmost love and gratitude, thanks to all of you above for being there when I needed you the most. You will always be in my heart.

Finally, to my publicist and manager Robbi Gunter, for urging me to bust this material out of the archives, to publish and share with potential readers seeking wisdom, solace, and a little humor. May this book offer hope, comfort, peace, encouragement, and direction.

Rebecca Bassham, BS, RT, BCN, BCB-HRV, QEEG-T
December, 2020

ABOUT THE AUTHOR

Rebecca Bassham is a health educator who after working as a medical imaging specialist seeing so much sickness and disease that it broke her heart, has committed her life to helping people to become healthier through lifestyle change. She is a graduate of CSUF's department of Exercise Science and minored in Health Promotions. She is a licensed Radiologic Technologist (ARRT) and completed a fellowship in CT and MRI at Loma Linda University. She invested 18 years as an entrepreneurial stay-at-home mother of three, which was the time she began to journal during quiet mornings with God. In 2010 she developed an interest in neuroscience that led her to board certification in Neurofeedback (BCN), Quantitative EEG technologist (QEEG-T), and HRV.

Rebecca has worked in the field of health and wellness for over 30 years with experience to include employee health, facilitating lifestyle change programs, promoting community health education and outreach through radio, television, email news campaigns, and establishing an organic produce distribution system in the desert of Arizona. Once she discovered the power of neurofeedback within her own family, she embarked on her studies of neuroscience in 2010.

After working in private practice, Edge NeuroFitness, specializing in cognitive enhancement, Rebecca became the Director of Neurosciences at Pure Sports Recovery, a holistic program that addresses the mind, body, and spirit. Most of her population includes former professional athletes. While she was never a professional athlete herself, she mastered the art of TBI recovery following several head injuries of her own that resulted from an appetite for adventure riding horses, dirt bikes, and bicycles. It was this experience that drove her passion to help people who were suffering. It was God who answered her prayers for healing, a venue, and career; a place to apply her collection of experience to help others as she helped herself. Stay tuned for her upcoming book, "Where Do I Go from Here? How to Get from Stressed to Blessed."

She is a BCIA-approved mentor for aspiring neurofeedback practitioners. Rebecca facilitates groups with life and wellness coaching to include brain fitness strategies, nutrition, exercise, goal setting, mindfulness, stress management, and time management for a holistic, alternative approach to improve cognitive function. She has also facilitated an equine-assisted learning program with her clients.

Contact Rebecca Bassham

Email:	bec@edgeneurofitness.com
Website:	www.edgeneurofitness.com
LinkedIn:	https://www.linkedin.com/in/beckybassham/
YouTube:	https://www.youtube.com/watch?v=ptMjaVRMZBo
Twitter:	https://twitter.com/edgeneuro
Instagram:	https://www.instagram.com/beckybraincoach/
Facebook:	https://www.facebook.com/becky.bassham.1
	https://www.facebook.com/Nutrition-For-Your-Soul-100388438582617
	https://www.facebook.com/EdgeNeuroFitness

CPSIA information can be obtained
at www.ICGtesting.com
Printed in the USA
FSHW012121160521
81509FS